CW00519889

STOLEN LIVES

Peter Lantos is a Fellow of the Academy of Medical Sciences and in his previous life he was an internationally known clinical neuroscientist who has retired from a Chair at the Institute of Psychiatry, King's College London. He is the author of numerous medical and scientific texts.

In retirement he has written a childhood memoir, *Parallel Lines*, published in London by by Arcadia Books in 2006. It was internationally acclaimed with four impressions, and was translated into Hungarian, Italian and German. This is the story of a boyhood journey from a sleepy provincial town in Hungary during the Second World War to the concentration camp in Bergen-Belsen. *Closed Horizon*, published in 2012, was his first novel: a story of loyalty and betrayal, guilt and forgiveness, blackmail and courage in the dystopic surveillance state of Britain of the near future.

His first three plays are collected in this volume. He is working on his fourth play, *Light and Shadow*, the story of an extraordinary love affair between the French painter, James (Jacques) Tissot and an Irish Catholic divorcee with an illegitimate child in the setting of Victorian high society.

Peter Lantos was born in Hungary and has been living in London for 50 years.

STOLEN LIVES

A trilogy of Hungarian Plays

by

PETER LANTOS

REGENT BOOKS
LONDON

First published in the United Kingdom by
Regent Books
11 Chester Place
London
NW1 4NB

peter.lantos@btinternet.com
www.peter-lantos.com

A catalogue record for this book is available from the British Library

ISBN 978–1-9999767-0-5

Designed and typeset in Minion Pro by Discript Limited, Chichester
Printed in Scotland by Bell & Bain Ltd

CONTENTS

Acknowledgments

I wish to thank Nina Steiger and Rebecca Lenkiewicz, two tutors of the Faber & Faber Writing Academy without whose enthusiasm and encouragement I would not have embarked on the utterly foolhardy endeavour of writing my first play in my early seventies after forty years in clinical neuroscience.

I gratefully acknowledge the help of Jeremy G. Connor, the late Peter Frisch and James Roose-Evans who made useful suggestions to the original scripts. My particular thanks are due to Bernard Krichefski, Carl Miller and Nicholas de Jongh for their professional advice.

Richard Bates not only edited the plays but also produced and designed this book, and for this I am grateful beyond words.

FOREWORD

I doubt there can be a dramatist, writing in the English language today, who endured an early childhood more terrifying than that of the originally Hungarian Peter Lantos. His three plays, all written since his retirement from King's College London's Institute of Psychiatry, where he had a chair of Neuropathology as clinical neuroscientist, all bear some measure of personal experience or perception of the terrors and political convulsions that afflicted his native country and some Hungarians in the mid and later years of the twentieth century. As far as English-speaking readers are concerned Lantos offers, therefore, what must rank as a unique commentary and perspective in theatrical form on a country rent asunder.

The Hungary that Lantos depicts in his plays swings between the lower depths of Hitler's anti-Semitic Fascism and the steely grip of Soviet Communism. But these are not plays with direct political themes. The right- and left-wing forces of absolutism ensure that Lantos's characters, living out their private, professional and domestic lives, resemble marionettes forced to dance to the tunes of the time. How did these prime victims of governing fanaticisms survive and at what cost? And for how much of their lives were they haunted and harrowed by their early years: *Stolen Years*, the last of the three in the volume, at first seems as effervescent as the champagne lavishly consumed by four friends reuniting to celebrate the decline and fall of Communist rule in 1989. But as with Ibsen's *Ghosts*, the spectres of the past finally rise up to reveal how the lives at least two of the celebrators have been irrevocably ruined by sexual fascism. The atmosphere in *The Visitor* is at first vaguely redolent of the atmosphere of a Chekhovian family, secure in prosperity. But anxiety and fear begin to seep into their lives, like a dangerous virus in the bloodstream: the play leaps chillingly beyond the confines of realism to issue a warning that no one fully appreciates. Death looms on the horizon and takes most of them.

This is the most autobiographical of Lantos's plays and the most shocking. It takes its theme straight from life. Born into fairly affluent Jewish circumstances during the early years of the Second World War, when the family timber business seemed an apparent emblem of financial security and respectability, the Lantos family were caught in the Nazi death trap. Shortly before his fifth birthday in 1944 Peter Lantos stood with his mother and father at a Hungarian railway station where some of the cattle-truck trains that arrived were scheduled to the deathly destination of Auschwitz: almost all the arrivals who survived the trip were almost at once marched away to the gas chambers. By a stroke of good luck the train onto which the Lantos family were crammed turned out to be destined for Bergen-Belsen. Here there were no gas chambers. The arrivals, according to Lantos's account in his great autobiographical reminiscence, *Parallel Lines*, published in 2006, merely endured what he termed 'hell on earth'. A commandant from Auschwitz had recently arrived and things got worse.

Thanks to this new regime, the lice-ridden inmates suffered no more than cruelty, disease and starvation. Death often followed on in the aftermath to these relative inhumanities. When Belsen was liberated by the British Army there were some 10,000 corpses. Peter and his mother, though not his father, were to survive Belsen and liberation by US forces from the train carrying them even deeper into Hitler's terrain. They were handed to The Red Army and having escaped from them eventually they returned to Hungary. The family business and their home gone, and most of their family had been slaughtered in the Holocaust.

I detail these harrowing sequences of autobiography and relate them to two of his plays in an effort to make a point about their oblique political nature. For more than 200 years in Britain a senior official of the Royal Household – the Lord Chamberlain – was charged with licensing all plays performed in professional theatres. He was a rigorous censor. He even banned *Oedipus Rex* in the early part of the twentieth century. Nothing could be staged before his office gave it his approval. Not until an Act of Parliament in 1968 did he cease to operate his form of reactionary, almost comical censorship. No plays that dealt with contemporary political characters or political problems had much of a chance of being approved for production. Terence Rattigan wrote a rather farcical play mocking Hitler – at least the dictator concerned was clearly Hitler but not so named. It was banned until war was declared in 1939. Then permission for performance was given as it did not matter any more that the play would give offence to Germany.

Because the UK theatre was so subject to censorship until 1968 it is hard to discover many British plays written and performed on the London stage, or anywhere beyond it in Britain, that dealt, for example, with the iniquities of the 1930s Depression, when Baldwin's and Chamberlain's Conservative governments imposed a form of austerity not dissimilar from that we suffer today. The process by which the long-term appeasement of Hitler was ended when Churchill finally secured his grip upon Prime Ministerial power only became the stuff of a theatre play a few years ago. Dodie Smith's sentimental *Dear Octopus* was doing good business as Neville Chamberlain came home from Germany in 1938 offering an imaginary peace in our time. The Octopus of the title referred to the way that the tentacles of this creature resembled those that bound comfortable, middle-class families together. A politically motivated and driven theatre could only take strong steps post 1968. Lantos's plays

introduce us to a politico-personal drama of Hungary's violent twentieth century times in a way that no other English-
speaking theatre writer has. It is worth reflecting on the fact
that if some Hungarian playwrights in the 1940s had aspired
to document the travails of his country in theatrical form
and found a translator, the Lord Chamberlain would probably have banned them.

© Nicholas de Jongh

Nicholas de Jongh is the former theatre critic of the *Evening
Standard*. His performed plays are *Plague over England*
(Finborough and Duchess), *The Unquiet Grave of Garcia
Lorca* (Drayton Arms) and *Pricked Out* (King's Head).

INTRODUCTION

The three plays collected in this volume form a trilogy. Although they carry messages from different ages, they have a common thread running through them. All three take place in Hungary against historical turning points: *The Visitor* from the introduction of anti-Jewish laws in 1938 to the Holocaust in 1944–1945, *Distorting Mirrors* from Stalin's death in 1953 to the Revolution three years later, and *Stolen Years* set on a single glorious day at the collapse of Communism in 1989.

More importantly, however, in all three the source of drama is the same human tragedy: an irredeemable conflict between vulnerable individuals and brutal authoritarian dictatorships, relentlessly motivated by an obnoxious ideology, be it Fascism or Communism. The characters are mostly outsiders or enemies, perceived or real, of 'the system' which corrupts, undermines and finally destroys them. They have the wrong religion or opposing political views, or simply their professional activity contradicts the prevailing dogma, or their love falls outside narrowly interpreted moral standards.

The Visitor chronicles the life and tribulations of a middle-class Jewish family, the Singers, between 1938 and 1945. Despite warnings from the mysterious Visitor, they are marched to their certain deaths, half-knowing but not admitting their immediate fate. Only the central character, Fanny, the matriarch of the family and her son, Leo, offer nominal resistance.

The play is based on the fate of my family. As a child of five, I was prisoner 8431 in Bergen-Belsen concentration camp where I was deported from a small provincial town in Hungary with my parents in the summer of 1944. Like the Singers of the play, most members of my family had perished.

In the closing scene Sarah and her young son arrive in the large family house devoid of life and barren of content – this is how I remember our return: a house, but not a home. My story is chronicled in my autobiography *Parallel Lines* published in 2006.

Distorting Mirrors faithfully reflects the fact that psychoanalysis was denounced as 'the private psychology of Imperialism' and banned under the Communist regime. The play follows the conundrum of Elsa, a leading psychoanalyst of the era. A Communist Party member herself, she has to renounce her own profession, but by continuing her practice clandestinely, she regains professional independence and personal integrity; only to lose everything in the end.

Studying medicine at the time in Hungary, it was painfully clear that even psychiatry was taught through the distorting influence of the all-pervading Communist dogma. It was not used as shamelessly as in the Soviet Union, where it was a weapon of oppression against the 'enemies' of the state. However, it was reduced to a secondary role to neurology, and many of the best practitioners of the subject had been purged from the textbooks and occasionally from life.

In *Stolen Years*, school friends who have not seen each other for some thirty years reunite in the late summer of 1989 in Budapest. They witness the collapse of Communism around them and relive the humiliation, cruelty and torture to which they had been subjected in the past. Whilst all the characters of *Stolen Years* are fictional, I experienced those febrile days in the late summer of 1989.

In 1970, I was sentenced *in absentia* to sixteen months of imprisonment and total confiscation of all my belongings for 'defection' to England in 1969. I have now my file held by the Hungarian State Security: it is quite an interesting read. I returned only twenty years later, on the auspicious day in September 1989 when the Hungarian government opened the border to Austria. This was the beginning of the end of

Communism: the Berlin Wall came down two month later in November. The elation of those days was felt by all, as if a poisonous gas had dissipated. However, at the same time the shadows of the past had emerged: accusations and recriminations for crimes, and the threatening revenge of punishing those who committed them; as if the dead could be revived and stunted lives repaired. 'The Communists stole forty years of our lives,' a friend said. And for that there is neither restitution, nor reparation.

What is the relevance, if any, of retelling events which happened in another country generations ago? Hungary is a particularly fertile soil for a crop of plays providing a changing historical backdrop. In these plays I aim to explore the antagonism between the vulnerability of the individual and the abuse of power by the state. In the twentieth century the country had a wide range of governance: a monarchy within the Austro-Hungarian Empire, a democratic and a Communist republic; a nominal kingdom ruled by a Regent with increasingly right-wing governments, a Fascist dictatorship, and then forty years of one-party Communist rule.

The plays in this volume cover a timespan of fifty years of the last century from 1938 to 1989. In our age when intolerance, prejudice and xenophobia still exist, these plays speak to the people of today, not only in Hungary but around the world.

Peter Lantos
London, 1 January 2018

THE VISITOR

CHARACTERS

FANNY, the Matriarch (56 years old)

Her children:

    SARA (31)

    SERENA (25)

    ANNA (21)

    LEO (32)

ALEXANDER, Sara's husband (44)

ADAM, Sara and Alexander's son (new born)

MARIA, the maid (16)

THE VISITOR

THE MAYOR

THE OFFICER

2 GENDARMES

The first act takes place in May 1938 in a provincial town in Hungary.

The second act starts six years later, soon after the country's invasion by German troops in March 1944.

The epilogue unfolds in the early autumn of 1945.

ACT ONE

The dining room of an upper-middle-class family home. Upstage, there is a door, which leads to the entrance hall; on one side of the room another door opens into the kitchen and on the opposite side a double door leads into the drawing room. Both the drawing room and the kitchen can also be accessed directly from the hall. When the door to the hall is opened, it may be possible to glimpse the foot of a staircase, which leads upstairs to the first floor of the house and when the door to the drawing room is opened, there may be evidence of elegant but comfortable furniture: bookshelves and part of a grand piano may also be visible. The dining room itself is simply but elegantly furnished. The large dining table is surrounded by eight antique chairs: three on each side, one at the end and a carver's chair at the head of the table. There is a large Persian rug under the table, and an imposing sideboard against the wall on which two oil portraits hang: Fanny's and her husband's, Samuel's. There is also at least one small armchair. The room is empty until . . .

FANNY, *a woman in her fifties, with immaculately coiffed silver hair, lived-in face but perfect posture, wearing a simple but smart skirt with a cardigan and blouse, enters from the hall. She crosses the room, removes the two large silver candlesticks from the end and the flower arrangement from the centre of the dining table, and places them on the sideboard. She opens the sideboard.*

FANNY. Where is the special tablecloth? I hope it's starched and ironed properly. Here it is. (*She takes out a large, folded linen table cloth and begins to spread the cloth over the table, carefully smoothing it as she goes along.*)

(MARIA *enters from the kitchen.*)

MARIA. Madam, can I help you? Please let me . . .

FANNY. Let's do the tablecloth together Maria and then I think I'd like to lay the table myself today. If you would just pass me the china, the glasses and the cutlery, then you can leave the rest to me. (*Silence.*) It's a special day today, Maria. (*Pause.*) Very special. Why don't you help Rose in the kitchen instead? She's going to be very busy.

MARIA. Yes, madam.

(*She disappears into the kitchen.*)

(FANNY *starts to arrange the china and cutlery on the table, starting at the head, while* LEO *enters the room from the hall and watches his mother. He is a tallish man in his early thirties, wearing a suit and a bow tie, with an overcoat loosely draped over his shoulders.*)

LEO. Always the same . . .

FANNY. 'The same?'

LEO. You know *exactly* what I mean.

(*Silence, during which* LEO *takes off his overcoat, throws it on the back of the armchair and lights a cigarette.*)

FANNY. Good walk?

LEO. Yes, thank you.

FANNY. Dr Krausz has just left.

LEO. What did he say? Is there anything new?

FANNY. Not really. The breathing is getting worse.

LEO. Mother, I'm sorry. I didn't mean to upset you.

FANNY. No, I don't suppose you did. (*Pause.*) With or without your approval, I will lay your father's place at table, as I've done for more than thirty years. I know he won't be coming down to eat with us today to celebrate. But while he lives and breathes under this roof, this is his place. Whether you like it or not.

(SERENA *enters from the kitchen, holding a bunch of lilac stems. She is a stunningly beautiful woman in her mid-twenties wearing a simple, well-cut dress. She kisses* FANNY *before proceeding to arrange the flowers in a vase on the side table.*)

SERENA. Isn't this a beautiful day? The scent of lilacs in the garden is so intoxicating! I just had to bring some in! I can't remember a spring day like this. Is anything wrong? Surely not today of all days? Is it father?

FANNY. Nothing is wrong, Serena. Nothing. Really.

SERENA. Wasn't the service marvellous? Dear little Adam! He hardly cried at all. And it seemed to be all over in seconds. Mind you, I'm pleased I wasn't born a boy.

FANNY. Where is Joseph?

SERENA. (*Hesitating.*) Oh, Joseph. I upset him. Or so he said. Don't worry; he'll be here for lunch.

FANNY. Leo, would you go upstairs for a few minutes to see how your father is? And take your coat with you, will you? That's what the cloakroom is for.

(LEO *leaves the room.*)

FANNY. Why does he never close the door behind him?

(SERENA *takes the hint and closes the door.*)

FANNY. I'll never understand you, Serena.

SERENA. Really, Mother?

FANNY. These quarrels! It isn't my imagination, is it?

(SERENA *remains silent.*)

FANNY. Serena, I'm talking to you.

SERENA. Yes, Mother . . .

FANNY. They're getting more and more frequent, aren't they? I wish you'd try to control yourself. He is such a decent man!

SERENA. Mother, *I* live with him. *I* know what he's like. (*Pause.*) Yes, he is decent. Terribly decent. And stubborn. Very stubborn. You just don't know . . .

FANNY. May I ask what you've been arguing about this time?

SERENA. No. You may not.

FANNY. Try to control your tone, Serena. I only want to help. You must know.

SERENA. Your help means, you want me to do as *you* would do. Not quite the same thing, is it?

FANNY. Probably not. Families . . . We all know each other so well and yet we understand each other so little.

(*The front door bell rings.*)

FANNY. Please try to remember, my dear. To be married to a man like Joseph is a great blessing and you should never forget the vow you took to make him happy!

(MARIA *comes in from the hall with a letter in her hand.*)

MARIA. Madam . . .

FANNY. We've already had the morning post.

(MARIA *hands the letter to* FANNY, *then leaves to the kitchen.*)

SERENA. Special delivery?

FANNY. Addressed to Leo.

SERENA. Who's it from?

FANNY. I don't know. (She *hands it to* SERENA.)

SERENA. I wonder. (*She opens the door into the hall and calls upstairs.*) Leo! Express letter for you.

LEO. (*Off.*) I'm coming. (*Enters the dining room.*) Where is it?

SERENA. (*Handing him the letter.*) Sender unknown!

FANNY. How is your father?

LEO. (*Absentminded.*) His breathing's got noisier.

FANNY. I'll go up.

SERENA. Mother, you can't be at father's bedside all the time. The nurse knows what she's doing.

FANNY. I've been at his side all my adult life, Serena. I may not be able to accompany him where he's going, but at least I can be with him until then. (*Pause.*) And that may not be very long.

(FANNY *leaves the room.*)

SERENA. (*visibly moved and waiting for her mother to be out of hearing.*) I wish I could be more like Mother.

LEO. Thank God you aren't. It took five weeks before she stopped resenting the nurse. She may have stopped complaining about her, but she still doesn't trust her.

SERENA. Who's it from?

LEO. Can't you mind your own business, just for once?

SERENA. Touchy!

LEO. Don't be childish. (*Opens the letter and, as he reads it, his disappointment becomes palpable.*)

SERENA. Bad news?

LEO. No . . . Nothing . . . not really . . .

SERENA. Leo, come on! It's written all over your face. Why won't you tell me?

(*With a sudden move* SERENA *grabs the letter from* LEO's *hand and darts round to the other side of the table to try to read it.*)

LEO. (*Tries to chase her, only giving up when he knocks over a chair.*) Serena!

SERENA. (*Astonished*) I don't believe it! That you could have even considered it. Are you serious?

LEO. Mind your own bloody business. Father's not going to die . . . yet. He may go on like this for months!

(ANNA *rushes in from the hall. A young woman just over twenty, she is very pretty and full of youthful energy. She wears a spring dress with a light jacket, and carries a music satchel.*)

ANNA. Hello, you two . . . (*Looking at the overturned chair.*) What's been going on here? Anyway, how did it all go? I wish I could have been there! Gosh, I'm famished. I must get something to eat! Back in a minute!

(ANNA *disappears into the kitchen.*)

LEO. (*Calmer.*) Give me the letter!

(SERENA *hands the letter back to* LEO, *watched by* FANNY, *as she comes back from the hall. She goes to the overturned chair and, without comment, she rights it.*)

FANNY. What's going on?
LEO. (*looking pleadingly at* SERENA.) Nothing, we just . . .
FANNY. Is Anna back?
SERENA. Yes.
FANNY. Where is she?
LEO. She went to the kitchen. Starving, as usual . . .
FANNY. (*interrupts.*) How did it go at the Conservatoire?
LEO. She didn't say.
FANNY. You didn't ask?
SERENA. We didn't get much chance.
ANNA. (*Returns from the kitchen.*) Mother . . .
FANNY. (*interrupts.*) How did it go?
ANNA. Why is Maria crying in the kitchen?
FANNY. Is she? I saw her a few minutes ago, and she was fine.
SERENA. I wonder what upset her.
LEO. We could always try asking.
ANNA. I did. She wouldn't say . . .
FANNY. Let's see. (*She opens the kitchen door.*) Maria, please come in for a minute.
MARIA. (*Enters from the kitchen, visibly upset.*) Yes, Madam?
FANNY. What's happened?

(MARIA *remains silent.*)

FANNY. Anna said you were crying in the kitchen. Has Rose been unkind to you? Did she upset you?

MARIA. No Madam, not at all . . .

ANNA. (*Walks to Maria and takes her hand.*) Please, Maria, tell us what's going on!

MARIA. (*After pause gathers up her courage.*) Rose asked me to get some cinnamon sticks for her. (*Pause.*) On the way to the shop, I met a boy I was at school with. (*Pause.*) He's joined the gendarmes now. (*Pause.*) And he said . . . he said . . .

ANNA. What *did* he say?

MARIA. He asked why a nice girl like me is working for . . . working for . . . a family like yours.

(ALL *remain silent for a few second.*)

FANNY. (*Regaining her composure first.*) And what did you answer?

MARIA. I said it was none of his business . . . (*Hesitating.*) And I said I like working for you. That you're good to me.

LEO. Well done, Maria. Mother, if you'll excuse me . . . (LEO *goes into the drawing room, leaves the door open behind him.*)

FANNY. Was that all?

MARIA. (*Hesitating.*) No. He also said that if I wanted to be a maid, I should work for a proper Hungarian family. I replied that you *were* a Hungarian family and he just laughed. (*Pause.*) And when I said it's up to me to choose who I work for, he shouted at me that soon I'd change my tune.

FANNY. Thank you, Maria. You'd better go back to helping Rose. (MARIA *leaves the room.*) How did the Schubert go, darling?

ANNA. Very well, I think.

FANNY. Good, after all that practice!

ANNA. It's not official but they said I'd almost certainly be through to the next round.

FANNY. Isn't that marvellous? Well done, my dear.

SERENA. That's lovely! What a talented little sister we've got.

FANNY. Where has Leo disappeared? He'll want to hear your news.

SERENA. I think he just wants to read Max's letter in peace.

FANNY. Whose letter?

SERENA. Max. His friend. You know.

FANNY. Max? (*Pause.*) Oh, yes. I do! Funny boy! I've never understood what Leo sees in him!

SERENA. Mother, you don't need to know everything.

FANNY. There's something about him . . .

ANNA. He's very fond of Leo. (*Pause.*) Mother, actually something else happened this morning. Rather strange . . .

FANNY. What?

ANNA. A boy in the class above mine, who is studying violin, came up to me just after I'd finished playing.

FANNY. Yes . . .

ANNA. Why are you both looking at me like that?

SERENA. Go on!

ANNA. He said . . . (*Pause.*) It was so funny. I thought, at first, I hadn't heard him properly. But then, he said it again and I couldn't quite believe that he . . . that he'd . . . said it at all . . .

SERENA. For God's sake, are you going to tell us or not?

ANNA. Yes. Yes, I am. (*Pause.*) He said: 'I want to spend the rest of my life with you.'

FANNY. He wants to spend the rest of his life with you? (*Pause.*) Does he *know* you?

SERENA. The Schubert certainly hit the right note!

FANNY. What's his name?

ANNA. Daniel . . .

SERENA. Oh, so he's . . .?

ANNA. His father's a priest.

(*Silence.*)

SERENA. Ah . . .!

FANNY. What sort of priest?

SERENA. Well he's hardly likely to be a Catholic priest, is he? Not with a son. Unless, of course . . .

ANNA. No, a Protestant priest . . . (*Pause.*) His father is a Protestant priest.

FANNY. A Protestant priest!

ANNA. Yes . . .

SERENA. I believe they are known as pastors.

FANNY. Does it matter what they are called?

SERENA. Well, now we know, don't we? Anna has an admirer who is the son of a Protestant priest.

FANNY. I'm speechless.

SERENA. No, you're not Mother. And it's not as if they've run away together. He isn't Anna's husband. Not yet, anyway. (*Pause.*) Maybe he never will be.

ANNA. Thank you for that, Serena.

FANNY. What did you say to him?

ANNA. That he shouldn't make jokes. But he said he wasn't. And then . . . I knew he wasn't joking. (*Pause.*) Of course I'd met him before, but today was different.

SERENA. Do you like him, Anna?

ANNA. (*Without hesitation.*) Yes, I do. (*Pause.*) He plays terribly well . . . (*Pause.*) And he has lovely eyes and beautiful hands. (*Pause.*) He asked whether, when the competition is over, I'd choose some Brahms, one of the sonatas for violin and piano. For us to play together.

LEO. (*enters*) Brahms, the greatest of the romantics! Perfect!

SERENA. Anna has an admirer.

LEO. Sounds as it's all signed and sealed. Big celebration before summer's out?

FANNY. I don't understand. With your father, it took more than a year before 'love' was even mentioned. As for 'marriage' . . . That boy must be mad!

ANNA. Mother, we aren't married yet! We're going to play

music together. That's all. For the time being. (*Pause.*) Can I ask him to visit us?

FANNY. (*Reluctantly.*) Perhaps . . . When your father is a little better. Maybe you should go up to see him now, but for God's sake, don't tell him that piece of news!

ANNA. Do you remember the colouring books we had when we were children? With black outlines we had to fill in with colours. You know what? Today, I feel as if I can see all the colours in the world, all at the same time.

(ANNA *rushes off into the hall.*)

FANNY. I am amazed!

SERENA. Bit of a surprise. You always said you were worried she was going to devote her life to music and end up a lonely spinster.

FANNY. Would you have married Joseph if he had not been . . . suitable?

SERENA. Ah yes . . . 'Suitable'. Yes, I would. (*Pause.*) What about you and father?

FANNY. Had he not been, I don't suppose I'd even have met him.

LEO. And now it's Daniel's family who'll be wondering whether *she's* suitable.

SERENA. Why?

LEO. Well, of course she's attractive and bright and talented. But there are other things they worry about nowadays, aren't there?

FANNY. I don't know what you're talking about. Are you saying your sister isn't good enough for a pastor's son?

LEO. Mother, you didn't take in a single word of what Maria was trying to tell you, did you?

MARIA. (*Entering the room from the kitchen.*) Madam, Rose is asking for you in the kitchen.

(FANNY *and* MARIA *leave the room.*)

SERENA. Don't take your mood out on her.

LEO. (*Lights a cigarette.*) She can be so blinkered.

SERENA. She's got her own problems, Leo.

LEO. This idea that father can hear anything you say to him, for a start. 'Don't tell him *that* piece of news.' He's unconscious for God's sake!

SERENA. Did Max give any reason?

LEO. He says he's met a girl . . .

SERENA. (*Bursts out laughing.*) And you believe him?

LEO. (*Irritated.*) I don't know.

SERENA. Max . . . I always thought he was the most beautiful boy in town. Blue eyes you could swim in. And I'd have killed for that wavy blond hair. All the girls in the class were in love with him. Are you very disappointed?

LEO. Playing gooseberry wouldn't have been much fun, would it? (*Pause.*) If it is that.

SERENA. You like Max a lot, don't you?

LEO. He was my best friend.

SERENA. Was?

LEO. Please, don't analyse every word I say.

SERENA. Never mind . . . Perhaps it's for the best. Not the wisest time to travel now.

LEO. I wanted to see Paris. That's all. We'd been planning this trip for months. (*Pause.*) I know it's silly, but it feels like if I don't go now, I never will.

SERENA. So, it's just about Paris, is it? Nothing to do with Max?

(LEO *doesn't respond.*)

SERENA. I gather the news from Dr Krausz wasn't too optimistic.

LEO. Once father's dead, that'll be it. I'll never get away.

SERENA. Perhaps you should go now.

LEO. On my own?

SERENA. We'll manage here and Alexander can keep things going at the factory, can't he? (*Pause.*) Can he?

(LEO *pulls a face.*)

SERENA. I thought he was a reasonably competent accountant.

(SERENA *and* LEO *look at each other and, relieved to be able to change the subject burst into laughter as . . .*)

(SARA *and* ALEXANDER *enter from the hall.* SARA *is holding the baby in her arms, while* ALEXANDER *is wheeling an empty pram.* SARA *is a woman in her early thirties.* ALEXANDER *is more than ten years older than his wife. His suit and tie are rather duller than Leo's and he wears glasses.*)

ALEXANDER. Hello everybody!
SARA. (*Reserved.*) What is so funny?
SERENA. (*Ignoring her question*) And here's the guest of honour. How is he after this morning's little ritual? He's really gorgeous, Sara.
SARA. Where's mother?
SERENA. In the kitchen. I'll get her. Mother, your grandson's arrived!

(ALEXANDER *eyes* LEO *uncomfortably, while* SARA *busies herself with the baby.* FANNY *returns from the kitchen and goes straight to* SARA, *who kisses her mother.*)

FANNY. (*Takes the baby in her arms, talking to him.*) Isn't he beautiful? My beautiful little grandson. He's definitely got your eyes, Sara.
LEO. (*Who hasn't so far shown much interest in his nephew, looks at the baby.*) You remember the gardener we all thought was so marvellous last year until he suddenly disappeared. *He* had beautiful eyes.
ALEXANDER. (*Lights a cigarette.*) Very funny Leo.

FANNY. (*To the baby.*) Let's go upstairs and show you to your grandfather. He's been waiting for you all morning.

(LEO *sighs and glances at* SERENA *with an ironic smile.*)

FANNY. Perhaps you should come too, Alexander. I'm sure you'd like to show your son off to his grandfather, wouldn't you? I can't remember when you last went up to see Samuel.

(FANNY, *with* ADAM *in her arms, leaves the dining room, followed, a bit reluctantly, by Alexander.*)

LEO. I'm going to do a spot of work before lunch. (*Glancing at Serena as he goes.*) After all, the factory won't run itself. Will it?

(LEO *leaves through the drawing room door. But even before he leaves the room, he pulls Max's letter from his pocket.*)

SARA. What were you laughing at?
SERENA. When?
SARA. When we came in.
SERENA. I've no idea. Can't remember.
SARA. I wish Leo wouldn't say things like that. It only upsets Alexander.
SERENA. Oh, come on, it was a joke. The whole world knows you'd never stray. Certainly not with a gardener!
SARA. Where's your husband? A new baby in the Singer family not worthy of Joseph's attention?
SERENA. Not at all . . .
SARA. So what?
SERENA. All right, if you have to know. We had a little argument.
SARA. 'Little'?
SERENA. Well . . . Pretty big actually . . .
SARA. When?
SERENA. As soon as we got home after Adam's circumcision.

SARA. (*Interrupting.*) I knew it. I told Alex. I could see there was something wrong. We should have asked him to be a godfather.

SERENA. No, Sara, it wasn't that. (*Pause.*) If you have to know, he's jealous of Alexander.

SARA. Joseph?

SERENA. Yes. Joseph.

SARA. Why? I don't understand!

SERENA. Joseph is desperate for us to have children.

SARA. And you're not?

SERENA. Of course I want children. (*Pause.*) But just not yet. It feels as if we've only arrived back from our honeymoon. I'm still young.

SARA. You're twenty-five.

SERENA. Which is hardly old, is it? I want to enjoy life before I get weighed down with responsibilities. You know.

SARA. Not really.

SERENA. And to tell you the truth, I'm frightened of it. The whole idea of putting on all that weight, losing my figure . . .

SARA. Does mother know?

SERENA. About the row? Yes. Not the reason. Unless she's guessed.

SARA. She probably has. You know what she's like. Perhaps you should talk to her about it. After all, she did have four of her own.

SERENA. And you think she'd understand? You can just hear it, can't you? 'Oh, Serena, I don't know what gets into you.' (*Sara smiles.*) 'Look at Sara. Trying for so long. And then just when we were all losing hope . . .'

SARA/SERENA. (*both sisters in unison, laughing*) 'Like a miracle . . .'

(FANNY *enters.*)

FANNY. We've put little Adam down into his crib in your old room Sara.

SERENA. I'm dying for a coffee.

FANNY. I'll get Maria to bring you some.

SERENA. Don't bother, Mother. I'll get it myself.

FANNY. Try not to get . . .

SERENA. . . . under Rose's feet. Don't worry, I won't.

(SERENA *leaves for the kitchen.*)

FANNY. You know, Sara, I think your husband is going to be a very devoted father.

SARA. You sound surprised. Why?

FANNY. He said you wanted a word with me. But I think he just wanted to be left to look after his son.

SARA. I did want a word. But not now. It can wait.

FANNY. Are you sure?

SARA. Yes . . . No . . . maybe it can't . . .

FANNY. Not again?

(*Silence.*)

SARA. Yes.

FANNY. It can't go on Sara. You know that.

SARA. Yes. I do.

FANNY. How much?

SARA. Mother . . .

FANNY. Just say, how much?

SARA. Twelve hundred.

FANNY. Horses or cards?

SARA. Poker.

FANNY. Last time it was the wrong horse. This time I suppose it's the wrong cards.

SARA. He does win sometimes.

FANNY. Sara, spare me the details of your husband's gambling career.

SARA. It's not a career, Mother. No need to exaggerate.

FANNY. (*Ignoring her.*) I don't need a balance sheet to tell me he loses more than he ever wins. (*Pause.*) And you might as well know . . . It's not only the family who knows what's happening. I'm told tongues are wagging beyond this house, too. Alex isn't just your husband, Sara. He is the Chief Accountant of our company. He's in charge of all our finances.

SARA. Mother, this is a private matter. *Our* finances. Nothing to do with the business. (*Pause.*) He's been under a lot of pressure recently.

FANNY. In what way?

SARA. Oh, I don't know. Perhaps fatherhood . . . New responsibilities . . . He takes it all very seriously.

FANNY. Your father wouldn't approve of throwing away money like this. You know that, don't you?

SARA. I know.

FANNY. I can't go on paying Alexander's debts. Enough is enough! He has to learn.

SARA. I know.

FANNY. Then you'll understand that he has to live within his means. (*Pause.*) For the time being, the answer is no.

(*Silence.*)

SARA. (*Desperate now.*) Mother, please help me! I don't know which way to turn. I know Alex has to change . . . but what about me? (*Pause.*) And what's going to happen to Adam? What about your grandson?

FANNY. (*Angrily.*) Don't use your child to blackmail me!

SARA. (*Starts to cry.*) Mother . . .

FANNY. (*Surprised at the ferocity of her own response.*) Sara, I can't bear all this. It's not the day for it. And I'm not going to be rushed into a decision. Not today of all days! We'll discuss it later. (*With a deliberate effort to calm herself down, as well as* SARA.) We'll talk again soon. I promise, darling. (*Pause.*) But there is one thing. If I do see my way to helping you . . . to bailing Alexander out . . . it will be on one condition. The money will be paid to you, and not to your husband!

SARA. I understand, Mother.

FANNY. And while we are talking about your husband, you might tell him that I would have preferred him to talk to me directly rather than hiding behind your skirt.

SARA. He's ... he's ... very proud.

FANNY. Is he? Then he should know that gambling debts do nothing for a man's pride. They're more likely to lead to his humiliation.

SARA. Yes, Mother. (*Pause.* SARA *more relaxed now.*) Did father ... does father ... have any faults?

FANNY. Does he? Well ... Not really. (*Pause.*) He had his ways. From the beginning of our marriage there were little ... what would you call them? ... little ruses to keep them from me. But I soon found out ... and so did everybody else.

SARA. The Saturday cigarettes.

FANNY. He just couldn't do without, not even for one day of the week.

SARA. (*Remembering.*) Yes, that's right. Straight after lunch he used to sneak out to the outside toilet, thinking no one would notice.

FANNY. Your father never 'sneaked' about, my dear.

SARA. What would you call it then?

FANNY. I don't know. But when he came back in the house, you could always smell the tobacco on his breath.

SARA. You remember that time ... I don't think it was a Saturday, maybe it was one of the festivals, when the maid before Maria ... I can't remember her name ... found him fully dressed sitting on the lavatory seat in a cloud of cigarette smoke ... (*Both laugh.*) Poor girl, she was so confused, she came running into the drawing room instead of the kitchen and just stood there in front of us, not knowing what to say!

(ALEXANDER *enters from the hall, followed by* ANNA *with the baby in her arms.* LEO *appears a moment later from the drawing room and* SERENA *from the kitchen. They are all surprised to be walking into a room full of laughter.*)

SERENA. Sounds as if we've been missing some fun?

SARA. Oh, we were just remembering Father's Saturday cigarettes.

LEO. 'The phantom smoker in the outside privy!'

(*More laughter is interrupted by the sound of* ADAM'*s crying in* ANNA'*s arms.* ALEXANDER *takes the baby who continues to cry.*)

ALEXANDER. He wouldn't settle upstairs . . .

SARA. Probably needs feeding. Give him to me.

ALEXANDER. (*As he hands the baby to Sara, hoping that no one will hear.*) How did it go?

SARA. For God's sake Alex!

(*If* FANNY *has heard she shows no sign of having done so, but* LEO *and* SERENA *certainly have and they exchange looks, noticed by* ANNA.)

FANNY. (*Deliberately changing subject.*) So, I wonder if it is going to be your turn next, Serena?

SERENA. (*Pretending not to understand.*) What? To take baby Adam?

FANNY. You know exactly what I mean!

SERENA. Yes, Mother. I do. (*Pause.*) But not yet, I think.

LEO. In no hurry, then?

ANNA. I'm going to have lots of children . . . lots . . .

FANNY. Perhaps you should find a suitable husband first. Like Serena has.

LEO. Ah, yes, 'suitable'. Quite.

FANNY. I don't understand you, Serena.

SERENA. Really, Mother?

FANNY. Look at Sara and Alexander. Remember how long they had to wait?! And now like a miracle . . . making us all so happy.

(SARA *busies herself with* ADAM *to avoid meeting* SERENA'*s eye, making an effort not to giggle . . . and failing.* SERENA *does not even try to suppress her own laughter.*)

FANNY. Did I say something funny?

(*The moment is broken by the ringing of the front door bell.*)

FANNY. (*Surprised.*) Who would that be? Joseph has his own key, doesn't he Serena? We aren't expecting anybody else.
LEO. I'll go.

(LEO *sets off for the hall, leaving the door ajar so we can hear what follows.*)

LEO. (*Off, to* MARIA, *who is also on her way to answer the door.*) Don't worry Maria, I'll get it.

(*Members of the family wait apprehensively in silence and then listen to the exchange which follows* LEO'*s opening the front door to the new arrival.*)

THE MAYOR. (*Off.*) I wondered if I might have a few words with your mother, Leo. Forgive me for arriving unannounced.

(*Serena mouths the word 'The Mayor' to her mother, who stands stock still without responding.*)

LEO. (*Off.*) It's no trouble at all, Mayor. Do come through.

(LEO *shows* THE MAYOR *into the drawing room directly from the hall.*)

LEO. Please, sit down. I'll see whether my Mother's around.
THE MAYOR. (*Off.*) Thank you, Leo. I assure you, it won't take long.

(LEO *now reappears in the dining room, this time carefully closing the door behind him. The following exchange is not whispered, but they take care to speak quietly.*)

LEO. It's the Mayor.

FANNY. The Mayor? Why now?

LEO. He didn't say. Shall I show him in here?

FANNY. No, I'd rather go through.

ALEXANDER. What does he want?

LEO. I've got a pretty shrewd idea. And I wouldn't be too surprised if you have, too.

ALEXANDER. I don't know what you mean.

FANNY. Well, I suppose I should find out.

LEO. I don't think so, Mother. I think we should *all* find out.

(*And before* FANNY *can contradict him,* LEO *opens the double door and addresses* THE MAYOR *who has meanwhile been pacing restlessly up and down in the drawing room.*)

LEO. Please, do come through. We're all in here. As you know, today is a special family celebration.

(*After a moment* THE MAYOR *appears from the drawing room to find the whole family staring at him.*)

THE MAYOR. Yes, of course. Please allow me to offer you my warmest congratulations. (*Awkward silence before* THE MAYOR *greets each member of the family in turn.*) Mrs Singer, Serena, and the happy parents: Sara ... and Alexander. Ah and our young virtuoso, Anna too ... (*Looking at the baby in his mother's arms.*) Is this the new son and heir?

SARA. It is.

THE MAYOR. Does he have a name yet?

SARA. He's called Adam.

THE MAYOR. Ah, yes ...

SARA. Well, Adam was the first man; and he's my firstborn son. (*Pause.*) Forgive me, but I need to feed him.

THE MAYOR. (*He wants to get down to business.*) Of course, Sara. It's lovely to see you . . . and to meet Adam, of course. He's a fine looking baby.

SARA. Thank you. *She leaves the room.*

FANNY. (*Sitting down.*) Won't you sit?

THE MAYOR. May I ask first, if it isn't too painful subject . . . How is your husband?

FANNY. There is no improvement so far.

THE MAYOR. I'm very sorry.

FANNY. Thank you for your thought. (*Pause.*) But Mayor, this is a surprise! We were expecting you and your wife to have tea with us later this afternoon.

THE MAYOR. I know, dear lady . . . And I must apologise for this unannounced visit, but I'm sorry to say my wife and I aren't able to come this afternoon.

FANNY. Oh, I'm sorry to hear that, but couldn't you just have telephoned?

THE MAYOR. (*After pause.*) I wanted to see you in person, Mrs Singer because there is another pressing matter.

FANNY. Is this a social call or a business call?

THE MAYOR. It is both, Mrs Singer.

FANNY. Today we are celebrating the birth of our first grandson . . .

THE MAYOR. Yes, I know, but, as I say . . .

FANNY. 'Pressing'. Quite so. Nevertheless, it isn't the best time.

THE MAYOR. It's rather urgent. And quite important. For the whole family. Concerns have been expressed about the running of your firm. (*Pause.*) This needs to be addressed now.

FANNY. I'm not aware of any concerns.

ALEXANDER. What concerns, Mayor? As Chief Accountant, I think I'm entitled to know.

THE MAYOR. Well, it's not so much concerns as ...

LEO. ... new legislation.

(*This takes the room by surprise. Everybody, except Fanny, turns to look at him.*)

THE MAYOR. Yes, I thought you might have heard the rumours.

SERENA. You sound rather mysterious.

THE MAYOR. They've been circulating for some time.

FANNY. What rumours?

THE MAYOR. About the role in public life, and, I'm afraid, in business too of ... (*Pause.*) ... certain citizens of our town ...

ANNA. What 'citizens of our town'?

SERENA. Why don't you tell us Mayor?

THE MAYOR. Well ... How shall I put it? It's a little delicate this, I'm afraid.

LEO. It is not 'delicate' at all, Mayor. (*Pause.*) You're talking about Jews. Not to put too fine a point on it: us!

THE MAYOR. (*Ignoring* LEO.) New regulations are to be brought into force. The first will be published in the Government's official gazette tomorrow. (*Pause.*) And further legislation will undoubtedly follow.

FANNY. And what exactly will be published?

THE MAYOR. The participation of Jews in public life is to be restricted. (*Pause.*) The number of Jews in public offices, in the professions, like medicine and the law, in journalism, and in entertainment should not exceed their proportion in the population. And that is just about six per cent. (*Long pause.*)

LEO. How very interesting. I'm sure we'd all like to know where you stand on this. As Mayor, do you think six per cent a fair quota?

THE MAYOR. I can't say I do. But the fact remains that Jews

now occupy about one-third of the jobs in these areas, and many feel that that's not right.

(*The room is silent. Fanny gets to her feet.*)

FANNY. I thought, Mayor, that you were a friend of this family.

THE MAYOR. (*Following suit.*) Yes, Mrs Singer, I'm proud to say, I am. I supported your husband's nomination as a member of the town council. You may remember there was much opposition at the time. And later, when a couple of members wanted to deprive him of his membership of the Country Club, I was strongly against such a move.

FANNY. Perhaps you'll tell me then – as a friend, of course – why you and your wife aren't coming to tea this afternoon?

THE MAYOR. (*Uncomfortable.*) I've got to take public opinion into account.

FANNY. Quite. (*Pause. The Mayor now wishes the ground would open up beneath him.*) Then why exactly are you here now?

THE MAYOR. Could we talk in private?

FANNY. I don't have secrets from my family. Alexander is our Chief Accountant and, since my husband's illness, Leo has been in charge of the firm.

THE MAYOR. I know. But I believe that it is you and you alone who currently have sole control over your husband's business affairs.

LEO. (*Now abandoning his carefully cultivated ironic detachment.*) Does public opinion require you to root around in our private family arrangements, Mayor?

THE MAYOR. (*Defiant.*) The administration of one of this town's most important businesses is hardly a private matter, Leo. I'm afraid I would still prefer to talk to your mother alone.

FANNY. (*To cool the heated atmosphere.*) Very well . . .

LEO. Mother . . .

FANNY. It's all right, Leo. The Mayor and I will continue this conversation in the drawing room.

LEO. Please, let me join you.

FANNY. No, Leo.

(FANNY *leaves the room with* THE MAYOR. *Sara appears from the hall with the baby.*)

SARA. Has the Mayor left?

SERENA. (*Speaking quietly.*) He's next door with Mother.

ALEXANDER. The Mayor wanted to talk to your Mother in private.

SARA. Why?

ANNA. I don't understand what's going on.

SERENA. I'm not sure any of us do.

LEO. Will you tell them, Alex. Or shall I?

ALEXANDER. (*hesitant*) Interest has been expressed in the firm.

SARA. What sort of interest?

SERENA. You mean someone wants to buy it?

ALEXANDER. Possibly. There's been a lot of speculation. We've to open our books.

SERENA. Who to?

LEO. The local industrial co-operative. Owned, as they say, by 'the people'.

SARA. Couldn't we have refused?

LEO. No. The law is the law.

SERENA. Do 'the people' include the Mayor?

ALEXANDER. The Mayor is a shareholder and a director of the co-operative.

SERENA. Some friend of the family! The man's a turncoat.

ANNA. Mother will never agree to sell Singers. How would we live?

LEO. On the capital, the proceeds from the sale. We could live very well, believe me. (*Pause.*) If we sold it now. We could even leave the country.

ANNA. I don't want to leave the country!

SARA. And if we don't sell?

LEO. With this new legislation, we might be forced to sell later.

ALEXANDER. When the price might be much lower.

LEO. If there is a price at all.

SERENA. You mean they might just take it from us?

LEO. So you see Serena, he may not be so much a turncoat, as a saviour.

ALEXANDER. Well, I'd hardly award him a halo at this moment.

SERENA. (*interrupting*) Leo, I don't believe you.

ALEXANDER. Your brother is right, Serena. The Mayor, whatever you think of him – and I'm no keener than you are – is almost certainly throwing us a lifeline.

(*Fanny walks in from the hall, alone.*)

FANNY. (*referring to* ADAM) Shouldn't he be having a sleep?

SARA. He won't settle up there. I think he'll have to stay with us.

ALEXANDER. Let me.

FANNY. And now am I the only one who's hungry? Anna, darling, would you tell Rose that we're ready to eat?

(ANNA *goes towards the kitchen door but she's stopped by Leo.*)

LEO. Mother, you just can't leave us in suspense.

FANNY. I suppose not. Very well. The Mayor wants to buy the company. (*Silence.*) You don't seem surprised – any of you. I have to say I am.

SERENA. Leo told us.

FANNY. Leo did? What do you know of this, Leo?

LEO. The writing has been on the wall.

FANNY. What are you talking about?

LEO. There have been indications, Mother.

FANNY. 'Indications'? What sort of indications? And you chose not to share them with me?

LEO. I didn't know how to. Is it a good offer?

FANNY. The terms are not unreasonable.

SARA. What did you tell the Mayor, Mother?

FANNY. I told him I needed time to consider his offer. And also that I wanted to discuss it with my family. Does that surprise you, Leo? I imagined you might wish to express a view. Am I wrong?

LEO. (*hesitates*) I believe this may be our last chance, Mother.

FANNY. And the rest of you? Do you agree with Leo?

MARIA. Rose wants to know whether she should serve up, Madam.

FANNY. Not yet Maria. Could she wait a few minutes?

(MARIA *leaves the room. The silence continues until Fanny speaks again.*)

FANNY. I asked whether the rest of you agree with your brother. Will nobody answer me? Sara?

SARA. Leo made a strong case to us, Mother.

SERENA. He believes that in the end we may be forced to sell . . . or worse.

FANNY. Worse?

ANNA. They might just take it away from us.

ALEXANDER. (*looking up at last*) There may be no choice, Mrs Singer.

FANNY. I see. (*Pause.*) When my husband bought the firm Alexander, it was almost bankrupt. That's why he could afford it. The machinery was outdated and the business had been run down. The workers were demoralised. From week to week they didn't know whether they'd be paid. Often they weren't. Their families barely knew where their daily bread was coming from. And, until my children came along to keep me busy at home, I worked with my husband. We worked every hour God gave us to make this enterprise a success. (*Pause.*) Our friends told us we couldn't do it. But against all the odds, we did. We spent the best years of our lives building it up. We bought the most up-to-date machinery from Germany, equipment that had never been seen in this country. And our modest sawmill, this business, which Leo now wants to sell . . .

LEO. I don't *want* it, Mother. I fear we may have no choice.

FANNY. (*ignoring Leo.*) . . . this business grew into one of the largest timber merchants in the region. Samuel brought to this town prosperity of a sort it hadn't seen for years, And this is how the Mayor rewards us . . . With threats. (*Pause.*) Well, Leo, I don't believe he'll carry them out.

LEO. (*pleading*) Mother, look what the Nazis have been doing in Germany!

FANNY. Hungary is not Germany.

LEO. Not yet.

ANNA. Jews have been living in this country for centuries, Leo.

LEO. So they have in Germany.

FANNY. (*after a brief silence*) Just one more thing. There is someone you're all forgetting. Your father. This is not just my decision, or your decision, or our decision. Do we not have to take *his* opinion into account?

(*Unable to control his exasperation,* LEO *moves to a side table, bearing a silver cigarette box. He removes a cigarette and lights up.*)

FANNY. Kindly have the courtesy to hear me out, Leo? Contrary to what you believe, I do know that we can't consult him. (*Pause.*) We shall never consult your father again. He's slipping away from us. I know that as well as you. But do you really think we never discussed the situation before this stroke? Do you think I am so stupid, so blind that I haven't seen what is happening all around us? Your father believes – believed – that these terrible times will come to

an end. In the meantime, we must hold our nerve. We are
not the sort of people who run away. *Silence.* And now, I
think we should eat, don't you? Anna, would you please
tell Rose that we are ready?

(ANNA *goes off to the kitchen.* FANNY *takes her seat at one end
of the table and the rest of the family begin to move towards
the table to take their places.* ANNA *comes back from the
kitchen.*)

ANNA. There is a man at the kitchen door. He wants to come
in.
FANNY. (*showing her irritation*) It's getting like a railway sta-
tion in here. Does he want to see me?
ANNA. He says he wants to see baby Adam?
FANNY. What for?
ANNA. I don't know.
LEO. What's he like Anna?
ANNA. Difficult to say really. A bit odd. He's got a little ruck-
sack on his back.
SERENA. Can't he wait till after lunch?
SARA. What's his name?
ANNA. He didn't say.
SARA. We aren't letting some stranger into the house just
because he says he wants to see our baby. Alex, go and send
him away.

(ALEXANDER *makes for the kitchen, but, before he even gets to
the door, he is stopped by the entry of* THE VISITOR *from the
kitchen. He is a man of indeterminate age but his beard makes
him look older than he is. His clothes are worn, like those of a
traveller who has been on the road for a long time.*)

THE VISITOR. Good afternoon.
FANNY. (*getting to her feet*) Good afternoon. (*Pause.*) I don't
believe we know you, do we? Have we met before? Forgive
me, but who are you?

THE VISITOR. I am not from these parts and my name is of no consequence. I am who I am. What matters is who you are. You are Fanny Singer, the wife – soon, I fear, to be widow – of Samuel Singer. And these are your children: Sara, Serena, Anna and Leo. This is Alexander, Sara's husband, and the baby whom I have come to visit . . . is Adam, their son. Am I right?

(*The family is mesmerised.*)

LEO. (*after a silence*) Can you tell us at least *how* you know us?

THE VISITOR. I do not know you. Not in the real sense of the word. (*Pause.*) I know *of* you.

ANNA. Are you a police spy?

THE VISITOR. (*smiling*) No, I am not a spy, Anna.

SERENA. Then how otherwise would you know our names and where to find us?

THE VISITOR. There was no need for anybody to tell me who you are. Or that your baby nephew, Adam was born exactly eight days ago.

SARA. How do you know that?

LEO. Mother put an announcement in the local paper.

THE VISITOR. I did not read the local paper. It was his circumcision today. The eighth day after his birth. (*Pause.*) And I have brought him a little gift.

SARA. (*surprised*) That is very kind. (*Pause.*) But why? You don't know our son either.

THE VISITOR. Yes, I do. I will know your son for the rest of his life.

ALEXANDER. I'm sorry, but none of this makes any sense.

THE VISITOR. One day it might do.

LEO. The man is deranged. Can't you see that?

ANNA. I don't think a stranger who offers you kindness unexpectedly is necessarily mad.

FANNY. Anna's right. And it is hardly polite to refuse a present.

SARA. May I ask what it is?

THE VISITOR. (*produces a small box from his rucksack*) It is a silver goblet. It was used for the first time nearly two thousand years ago. For the wine we all bless on Sabbath Eve.

(THE VISITOR *hands the box to Alexander, who opens it.*)

ALEXANDER AND SARA. Thank you.

ALEXANDER. It's a Kiddush cup. The most beautiful Kiddush cup I've ever seen. (*He hands the goblet to Sara who holds it for a moment and then takes it to the pram as if to show it to the baby.*)

SARA. Look at his little hand. He's trying to touch it. I'm sure he can see it. Will it bring him luck? I hope it will.

THE VISITOR. It will. And he will need it. (*Pause.*) There will be war. War such as the world has never seen before - worse than any war before, worse than the last Great War. The four corners of the world will go up in flames. From England to Japan, from the Arctic Circle to Africa there will be war. And there will be weapons the world has never used before. There will be rockets which will reach targets hundreds and hundreds of miles away. And bombs that can destroy large cities and burn everything in their wake. People will smoulder into ash and buildings crumble into dust, leaving behind only shadows – and memories of shadows. There will be hatred on a scale the world has never experienced before. Whole peoples will be annihilated.

FANNY. Please don't go on. I can't bear this. Today we're celebrating with a ... (*she hesitates*) ... festive luncheon. Will you at least join us?

THE VISITOR. Thank you. There is no need. I must be on my way.

FANNY. The cup is very beautiful. It will be treasured. Thank you.

(THE VISITOR *starts towards the kitchen door.*)

FANNY. Anna, please show our visitor out, will you? And ask
Rose to give him some food for the road.

THE VISITOR. Many thanks to you, Mrs Singer. Goodbye.

(THE VISITOR *leaves with* ANNA. *Another silence. Nobody
knows what to say.* ANNA *returns.*)

ANNA. He's gone.

FANNY. We should eat, I think. But, if you will forgive me, I
would like to sit with your father for a few moments first.
Leo, I would appreciate it, if tomorrow morning you would
kindly go to the Town Hall and communicate my answer
to the Mayor. (*Pause.*) Tell him, that the Singers are not for
sale, and nor is their business.

(FANNY *leaves the room.* LEO *takes another cigarette from the
silver box and lights up without a single word. The rest of the
family starts to take their places at the table. They are interrupted by the telephone ringing in the hall.*)

ANNA. I'll go.

(*She goes out to the hall. The phone stops ringing and we can
hear her speaking, though not what she actually says. She
returns to the silent dining room.*)

ANNA. It was Joseph, Serena. He said he'd be here in a few
minutes.

SERENA. (*visibly relieved*) Thank you, darling.

(*Silence.*)

(*From upstairs there is a single heart-breaking cry, followed
by silence. In the dining room* SARA *and* SERENA *who are
already sitting at the table, rise and take each other's hand.*
LEO *takes* ANNA *in his arms.* ALEXANDER *stays at the table,
frozen. Soon after,* FANNY *can be heard coming slowly down*

*the stairs. Then she appears in the open door and standing
motionless, looks at her family. She says nothing but she does
not need to.* ANNA *rushes to her, followed by* SERENA. *They
each hold her, but she stands upright, silently dignified in her
grief.* ALEXANDER *gets to his feet and takes* SARA *in his arms.*
LEO, *isolated on his own, sinks into the armchair near where
he has been standing. The door from the kitchen opens and*
MARIA *appears. She is weeping.*)

ACT TWO

Six years later.

LEO *enters the dining room from the drawing room. He looks around, then makes for a gramophone sitting on a side table, lifts the lid, winds it up, and from a pile of records selects one, which he places on the turntable. The sound of a catchy, contemporary French chanson fills the room. Oblivious to his surrounding he starts to dance, holding his non-existent partner at arm's length.*

ANNA *enters from the hall. Dressed smartly for the occasion, she has lost some of her youthful effervescence. Seeing* LEO, *who ignores her and carries on dancing, she stops, surprised.*

ANNA. What are you doing?

LEO. What do you think?

ANNA. Tonight is hardly the occasion for dancing, is it?

LEO. And why not, Anna, darling, why not? Come on, be brave; let's have a twirl.

(*And giving* ANNA *no chance to object, he sweeps her of her feet, kicking the Persian rug out of the way.*)

ANNA. (*succumbs for a few moments before she breaks away from him*) Leo, I'm sorry. I'm really not in the mood. (*They stop.*) Still, it's a lovely tune. Where did you get the record?

LEO. I ordered it years ago. From Paris.

ANNA. Oh, yes. Paris . . . A little consolation, was it?

LEO. You could say so. Father didn't choose the best moment to leave us. Not very thoughtful of him, was it?

ANNA. Maybe you'll get there one day.

LEO. To Paris? Somehow I doubt it. Oh, it was just a dream. A little hallucination . . .

ANNA. Sometimes dreams, which don't come true, turn into nightmares.

35

LEO. (*wounded*) What? Like your marriage to Daniel?

ANNA. (*angry*) I hope you don't mean that. Comparing your stupid little fantasy of a trip to Paris with what's happened to Daniel . . .

LEO. (*Suddenly interrupts her*) Sorry. Sorry, sorry, sorry. Anna, darling, forgive me. Please. That was thoughtless. (*Pause.*) Will you forgive me? (*Pause.*) Let's just dance, shall we?

(*Reluctantly, she lets* LEO *sweep her off again.*)

ANNA. (*While in Leo's arms*) Leo, by the way . . .

LEO. Yes, sweetheart . . .

ANNA. I was passing your room, the door was open and I saw . . .

LEO. (*Stops, releasing Anna, annoyed*) What? Are you spying on me?

ANNA. Leo, don't be silly. Of course I wasn't.

LEO. Nosey little girl.

(*They fail to notice the kitchen door opened abruptly by* FANNY. *Seeing his mother, Leo pretends nothing has happened and resumes dancing with his reluctant sister.*)

FANNY. What on earth are you doing? (*Ignored, she raises her voice*) Turn that silly music off at once!

(*They hear her, but continue dancing.*)

ANNA. Leo, please stop.

(*They stop dancing, looking at Fanny.*)

FANNY. Leo, I don't want that stupid machine in the dining room!! Your father would never have put up with this!

LEO. (*Reluctantly stopped by his sister*) Father rather liked dancing, didn't he?

FANNY. Father knew what was proper and when!

LEO. (*Ignoring her*) And the 'stupid machine' is called a

gramophone. G-R-A-M-O-P-H-O-N-E! Welcome, to the twentieth century, Mother.

FANNY. (*Outraged*) I know what the machine's called! You really are out of your mind, Leo. Dancing . . . Tonight of all nights . . . Here in the dining room . . . Before dinner!

LEO. (*Mock outrage*) Dancing on the Eve of Passover! In the dining room! Before dinner! Members of the jury (LEO *bows towards an imaginary jury*), can there be any mitigating circumstance? None? In that case, I put it to you that 40 strokes of the lash is the minimum sentence possible.

FANNY. (*Ignoring him*) Where is Susie, Anna?

ANNA. Didn't Sara tell you? I'm so sorry, Mother. This afternoon, she suddenly developed a nasty cough with high temperature.

FANNY. Why are you not with her?

ANNA. Oh, Daniel's mother insisted on looking after her. (*Pause.*) Susie and her grandmother are inseparable. It's a love affair. Last week she rustled up one of Daniel's favourite childhood books from the attic. Grimm's fairy tales. Now Susie insists on granny reading it to her over and over again.

SARA. (*Wearing an apron over her dress enters from the kitchen*) Anna, you made it!

FANNY. Anna tells me she gave you a message for me, Sara.

SARA. (*Weary*) Yes. Susie's not well. I'm sorry, Mother. I forgot. Without Rose and Maria, I've had my hands full. What happened to the music? It was lovely.

FANNY. Your brother and sister were dancing in here.

SARA. Is it such a sin to have a bit of fun?

FANNY. I didn't ask for your opinion, Sara.

LEO. Where is your husband, Sara?

SARA. He's getting some horseradish for the Passover plate.

LEO. Digging it up on the racetrack?

(SARA *bends to straighten the rug that* LEO *kicked aside.*)

FANNY. Leave your sister alone. I don't know what gets into you, Leo. All you seem to want nowadays is to upset us all.

LEO. (*Lights a cigarette*) Well, I *seem* to be succeeding, don't I?

SARA. If you'd thrown yourself more wholeheartedly into the business after father died, maybe they wouldn't have taken it over.

LEO. That's utter rubbish, Sara. And you know it. I suggest you face up to the facts. To be precise only to one fact. (*Pause.*) Our firm, Samuel Singer and Family, is not ours any more. Painful it may be, but we have to learn to accept it.

ANNA. Stop, Leo!

SARA. Leo, I didn't mean to hurt you.

LEO. I've stopped. All right? Because you all know everything there is to know, don't you? You're sure about that, are you? Quite sure? (*Pause.*) So you must know I was officially – and unceremoniously – kicked out from the firm yesterday. You knew that, didn't you? (*Pause.*) Can you imagine how humiliating that was?

(*All remain silent.*)

LEO. Mother didn't tell you? (*Pause.*) I thought not.

SARA. (*to* FANNY) You knew?

FANNY. Yes, of course, I did.

SARA. What'll happen now? Who's going to run Singers?

LEO. Well, certainly not us. (*Pause.*) Earlier this week the mayor appointed the new director, a pen-pusher from the town hall. One of his cronies. Yesterday, he came to visit his new empire and prowled about as if he had already owned the place. (*Pause.*) The irony, of course, is that he does. Though he knows as much about running a timber yard with over a hundred employees as you do about the theory of relativity. Arrogant little bastard!

SARA. Leo, I'm really sorry. But you should have told us, shouldn't you?

LEO. I'm surprised Alex didn't tell you.

ANNA. Didn't you see today's paper? A report celebrating the takeover of our company: 'The end of profiteering by Jews heralds in a new era of the welfare and the protection of the general public.'

LEO. (*muttering*) 'Welfare and protection of the public,' my arse.

FANNY. Leo, do you mind?

LEO. I bet that they wreck the business within a couple of months.

FANNY. It's such a tragedy. It was . . .

LEO. Mother, we know the story, we've heard it over and over again!

FANNY. (*Ignoring* LEO) We devoted our best days, our whole life to its success . . .

LEO. (*Getting increasingly aggressive until he and Fanny are all but shouting at each other*) Yes – and was it worth it? Answer me.

FANNY. Of course it was! Where would we be without Singers? And where would this town be without it?

LEO. Has it ever crossed your mind that father's early death . . .

SARA. Leo, stop!

FANNY. Where do you think the money came from for your education?

LEO. . . . was precisely because he had to work like a slave . . .

FANNY. For your holidays? For your expensive clothes?

LEO. . . . . to pay off the bank loan?

FANNY. It was his sheer hard work, which made us the biggest timber merchants in the county.

LEO. Just answer my question, Mother! Was it worth it?

ANNA. Don't, Leo!

(*Silence.*)

FANNY. You want to know the truth? Now, that we've lost everything . . . (*Pause.*) No. It wasn't. It *wasn't* worth it.

SARA. But surely, Mother we haven't lost everything. They may have taken our business, but we still have . . .

LEO. (*interrupts*) For how long, I wonder.

FANNY. (*ignoring them*) All gone. Everything. It's a blessing your father isn't here to see it. It was his whole life's work. (*On the verge of breaking down, she turns away from her family and walks towards the kitchen*) I'm going to see to dinner.

(ALEXANDER *enters with* ADAM, *a boy of six, in tow, but* SARA *lays into him before he can utter a word.*

SARA. Where on earth have you been? I thought you were never coming!

ALEXANDER. Good evening everybody. I'm sorry, Sara, but it took an awfully long time to find any horseradish. Last year it was easy, but today I had to dig up half the garden. (*Triumphantly he produces a bunch of roots wrapped in paper and hands them to his wife*) Here it is!

SARA. (*Putting them on the sideboard*) Thank you.

LEO. (*Turning to* ALEXANDER). Success on the turf at last. Though sadly not on the turf that counts!

ALEXANDER. Drop it Leo!

SARA. (*Defending her husband*) Could you just leave off for once? (*Turning to* ANNA. Shall we lay the table? She walks to the sideboard, and produces a large, folded linen cloth. Quickly she removes the empty vase and the candle sticks and with Anna's help she spreads the cloth over the table and expertly smoothes the creases. She replaces the two candle sticks towards the head of the table.

LEO. (*Aggressively*) Don't try to shut me up! Your husband is gambling with our money! Just because he does it through

one of his Gentile friends, do you really think we don't all
know? And who has to settle his debts?

ALEXANDER. I thought Leo you would have the decency . . .
at least tonight . . . (*He storms out of the room.*)

(*Silence.*)

SARA. For Christ's sake, Leo . . .

LEO. I wouldn't say 'for Christ's sake'. Particularly not tonight.
(*Pause.*) After all, it isn't just the first night of Passover. In
case you haven't noticed, it's Good Friday, too.

SARA. (*Goes back to the sideboard and searches inside*) Where
are the napkins? Since Maria's gone nothing is the same. I
must ask Mother.

(SARA *leaves to the kitchen, picking up the bunch of
horseradish.*)

ANNA. (*Takes out a pile of plates of various sizes and cutlery
from the sideboard*) Leo, you shouldn't have . . . (*Pause.*)
Can I ask you something?

LEO. Why not?

ANNA. Do you plan . . .? (*As Sara returns from the kitchen
with a pile of napkins; she immediately stops, looking at Leo
who avoids eye contact with her sister.*)

SARA. Here they are! Mother's getting a bit forgetful these
days.

ANNA. Are you surprised?

SARA. Where is Adam?

ANNA. He can't be very far. He was here a minute ago.

(*They hear Adam hesitantly practising scales on the piano
next door.*)

LEO. The little maestro . . .

ANNA. (*Turning to* SARA) Your son is very musical. Did you
know? Hate to say but he's more talented than Susie.

SARA. You're so good to him. He enjoys going to your house

so much and playing with Susie. (*She crosses the room to open the door of the drawing room.*) Adam! No . . . first you close the lid . . . gently.

(ADAM *enters.* SARA *kisses the top of* ADAM's *head and begins to place the napkins on the table.*)

ADAM. (*Turning to his mother*) Mummy, why do we eat horseradish tonight? I don't like horseradish. It's very hot. It gets into my nose and eyes and makes me cry.

SARA. (*Still busy with arranging the plates and cutlery*) I'm sure your father explained it to you, darling. At Passover dinner, we eat a bitter herb, like horseradish to remind us the bitterness of the time when we were slaves in Egypt. And now, be a good boy, find your daddy and ask him very nicely to come back. (*Looking at* LEO.) Tell him, we all want to see him.

LEO. Yes, we do.

(ADAM *disappears and shortly he returns, holding his father's hand.*)

ANNA. Sara, shall I grate the horseradish?

SARA. Thanks for the offer Anna, but I think I'll do it. (SARAH *disappears in the kitchen.*)

(LEO *sits down. There is an uncomfortable silence in the room.*)

ANNA. (*Walks to the table, surveying it*) Even Sara is absent-minded today. She's put the napkins on the table before the plates. (*She collects the napkins and begins to place the plates on the table, stopping from time to time.*)

ALEXANDER. Have you heard the latest story? Adam, go and help mummy in the kitchen.

LEO. I try not to listen.

ALEXANDER. You know one of our neighbours, the Gross family? (*Pause.*) Yesterday, two men reeking of drink turned up at their house, and apparently accused them of...

ANNA. (*Looking up from the table*) Of what?

ALEXANDER. Of murdering a Christian child and hiding the body in the house.

ANNA. No!

ALEXANDER. Suddenly two policemen arrived on bicycles. (*Pause.*) Instead of coming to the family's rescue, they had a warrant to search the house for profiteering on the black market and hoarding food.

ANNA. Did they find anything?

LEO. Oh, Anna, what do you think?

ALEXANDER. Of course not! No murdered child, no mountains of hoarded food.

FANNY. (*Enters from the kitchen*) Is Serena here yet? What's happened to her? Why does she always, always have to be late?

ANNA. It's just too awful.

(*The front door can be heard opening and closing.*)

(SARA *enters with* ADAM. *She is carrying the ritual Passover plate with the parsley, lamb shank, sweet paste mixture and eggs, leaving the kitchen door open behind her.*)

SARA. That will be her. Adam, be an angel, and get the other plate with the matzos.

(ADAM *leaves the room and returns, carrying in both hands the other silver tray, and gives it to* SARA *who places it on the table.*)

(SERENA *enters, wearing a hat and a pair of gloves, everything about her exudes glamour. Everyone gazes at her.*)

SERENA. Have you been talking about me?

LEO. Yes, of course, darling girl. What else would we be talking about? The rapid advance of the Red Army? When and

where the British and the Americans are finally going to get
off their arse and open the Second Front, which just might
save our lives? We could, even, just possibly, have been
discussing yesterday's new regulations and the disconnec-
tion of our telephones. Handed in your radio, have you?
No more BBC World Service, so now not even a modicum
of truth to counteract the government's rabid propaganda. There's a topic we might have been mulling over. And
then again, what about the list, published a few days ago?
The very short – though very precise list I may say – of the
clothing we're going to be allowed to take with us into the
ghetto. But no, darling, why would we waste time on such
trivialities when we can be talking about you?

(SARA *and* ANNA *busy themselves around the table with the
remaining crockery and cutlery.*)

ANNA. Leo!
SERENA. (*Unfazed, slowly removing her hat and gloves, while
the others watch her.*) You're on good form tonight, Leo.

(SERENA *proceeds to light a cigarette, which she inserts into a
long holder, but before she can light it,* FANNY *shouts at her:*)

FANNY. Serena, put that cigarette away!
SERENA. You haven't lit the candles yet. Sabbath and Passover
aren't officially in yet.

(*Sheepishly* SERENA *replaces her cigarette into a silver case
and turns to her brother.*)

SERENA. God! What a reception! A fine way to welcome your
sister to the festive table, Leo! (*Pause.*) Why are you in such
a foul mood?
LEO. Which of your gentleman callers have you been entertaining this afternoon? We're all dying to know. The banker with the money or the doctor with the wife? There'd be
no contest, would there, if only the banker wasn't twice

your age? (*He takes out a coin from his pocket, throws it into the air and catches it*) Rich banker, heads; poor doctor, tails. (*Looks at the coin on the back of his hand*) Surprise, surprise: rich banker.

FANNY. What is your brother talking about? (*Since no reply*) What are you talking about, Leo?

(*Long pause.*)

LEO. Come on Serena, why not tell Mother . . .?

FANNY. For God's sake. Is anybody going to tell me what this is all about?

LEO. (*When* SERENA *remains silent*) . . . that you've come from entertaining your banker friend, who should probably remain nameless, but whose initials might just be J.K. who visits you in your flat – frequently.

SARA. (*With amazement*) Not *him*?

SERENA. What's wrong with that?

FANNY. Serena, you aren't really saying that you've been entertaining a widower in your flat with nobody else present?

ANNA. (*Trying to help her sister*) Mother, Serena just . . .

SERENA. (*Now defiantly*) Anna, please leave this to me. (*Pause.*) Yes, Mother, that's exactly what's happening. (*Pause.*) What harm does it do to anyone if we have tea and a little civilised conversation?

LEO. Ah, but there is a little more to it than that, isn't there?

SARA. Leo!

LEO. Rather more than 'civilised conversation' over a cup of tea? (*Pause.*) You're having an affair with him. Aren't you? (*Pause.*) True or false that our sister is screwing an old man?

SARA. Leo, how dare you talk like that in front of mother!

LEO. (*Ignoring* SARA's *intervention*) And how does our sister come by all this new finery? That dress? The hat! The gloves! Are we supposed to believe Mother's allowance covers it?

ALEXANDER. Leo, are you out of your mind? This is hardly

the time and place for an inquisition into Serena's private life. And certainly not in front of a child! (*He takes* ADAM's *hand and drags him out of the room*) Come on Adam, let's go for a little walk in the garden. Let's see whether the storks are back.

ADAM. (*Off*) Daddy, what does the banker do to Auntie Serena?

LEO. (*Shouts after them as they disappear into the hall*) Something grown-ups get up to, Adam, when they haven't got anything better to do! (*Quietly, after the front door has slammed behind them*) He'll know it before long. That boy is nothing if not precocious.

SERENA. It's none of your business where I get my money from! Instead of getting at me, maybe you should take a look at your own miserable life! Just ask yourself one thing. (*Pause.*) You're thirty-eight and you haven't had a single regular girlfriend? Why would that be, I wonder?

LEO. Shut up, Serena!

SERENA. (*determined to continue*) Why should I? An eligible bachelor. Handsome and from a good family. With a bit of money. Why's that? Don't you fancy girls, Leo? (*Pause.*) There are enough nice, 'suitable' Jewish girls, around, aren't there? You could fill half the synagogue with them! Maybe your temper frightens them off? Is that it? And anyway, why are you so angry and malicious all the time? Is it frustration – because you don't have anyone special in your life? (*Pause.*) Well, if you want to know: yes, I am having an affair! (*They all look at* SERENA, *horrified.*) And I'll tell you something else. I'm enjoying every minute of it! Why shouldn't I? He's good company, he's intelligent and he's generous. Yes, he buys me presents. What's wrong with that?

LEO. You're a slut!

ALEXANDER. (*Returns from the hall with* ADAM.) Not still at it?

FANNY. Leo, don't ever use that word about your sister! Not even if all the dreadful things I've just been hearing were true. (*Pause.*) Are they, Serena? Answer me, will you!

SERENA. (*After a moment silence*) Yes, mother. They're true.

FANNY. You are a married woman! You have a husband at the front!

SERENA. I *had* a husband! Joseph was taken to Russia two years ago! Two bloody, miserable, lonely years ago! (*Pause.*) Do you really think he's survived? (*No one answers.*) Do you?

FANNY. I don't know, darling.

SERENA. Shall I spell it out to you?

LEO. Spare us.

ALEXANDER. It was a bloody disgrace – sending badly trained, ill-equipped soldiers to their certain deaths!

SERENA. But there were just a few who were lucky enough to be spared! Weren't there, Alex?

ALEXANDER. I was too old to be conscripted.

SERENA. Ah, yes. Of course, you were. Too old . . . Leo wasn't too old. But, of course, he had his 'heart condition'.

SARA. That's spiteful, Serena! Would it have helped if they'd taken Alexander and Leo away, too?

LEO. I've had enough of this. Alex, come with me! It's suffocating in here. (*Seeing* ALEXANDER's *surprise*) I'm sorry . . .

ALEXANDER. Never mind.

SARA. Don't be long . . .

(*Leo and Alexander leave the room.*)

SARA. (*Noticing Adam standing idle*) Adam, are you bored? I'll get your favourite book Auntie Anna gave you for your last birthday.

(SARA *leaves the room and returns with a book in her hand, which she gives to* ADAM *who with his mother's help sits on one of the dining chairs turning the pages of the book open on his knees. She joins* ANNA *at laying the table.*)

SERENA. I was devastated when he was taken away . . .

ANNA. I know the feeling all too well . . .

SERENA. . . . but I'm still young and I'm not prepared to be buried alive. (*Pause.*) Life, as we've known it, is coming to an end.

FANNY. What you are now doing is immoral.

SARA. Mother, please stop. Not in front of Adam.

FANNY. Look at Anna! Daniel was called up too. But Anna hasn't had an affair.

ANNA. I *know* what happened to my husband. (*She breaks down, sobbing.*)

(FANNY *goes to her and takes her in her arms.*)

SERENA. Anna has a daughter to look after. She doesn't sit alone in her house, day after day; waiting for a letter she knows is never going to arrive. (*Pause.*) Do you know the feeling of terror, when you wake up in the middle of the night and find the space next to you empty? You want to touch the body, which used to give you so much pleasure and warmth and security – in vain! And the cruelty of those grey mornings when you wander around the empty rooms of a cold, silent, dead house – touching the chairs that haven't been moved an inch for weeks. (*Pause.*) And the lonely meals . . . Breakfasts are the worst – facing the day ahead on your own. I couldn't bear it any longer. You can't know what it feels like, Mother.

FANNY. I can, Serena. And I do. Believe me, I do.

SERENA. I hardly dare to admit it – even to myself – but it would be easier to know he'd died than to go on putting up with this endless, soul-destroying uncertainty.

FANNY. If only you'd had a child.

SERENA. If only . . . But we didn't. (*Pause.*) I was foolish and vain. I know.

SARA. It could have made all the difference.

SERENA. Well, thank you, Sara. You too! Now the chorus of

disapproval is complete. (*She turns against her sister*) It's like an echo, isn't it? Mother says something and a second later you parrot it. No wonder you are the favourite.

SARA. That's absurd. I never competed with you. I never even envied your beauty. Nor all your boyfriends trooping through the house. I accepted who I was a long time ago. I'm the practical one, the plain eldest sister. I'm just the one who gets things done.

ANNA. You're not plain, Sara.

SERENA. I'm sorry. If you only knew how much I wanted a child and how frightened I was and now . . . (*She breaks down*) . . . it's too late.

FANNY. Frightened of losing your figure.

ANNA. (*Embracing Serena*) I don't blame you, Serena. You're right. It's easier for me. I have Susie.

SERENA. And you *are* a musician. If only I had something useful to do.

ANNA. I still practise every day. Sometimes for hours on end. I imagine myself playing in front of an audience. To remind me of the old days. And when I played with Daniel . . . I so adored playing with him. Oh, we argued sometimes. Over our repertoire. For me it always had to be Schubert. And for him it was his beloved Brahms. As if any of that mattered.

SERENA. I remember the last recital you gave together. It was heartbreakingly beautiful.

ANNA. The G minor. I'll never forget that night. Daniel had just been called up to go to the eastern front with the Second Army. (*Pause.*) He left the following week. Soon after, I was ordered off the podium.

FANNY. Anna darling . . .

SARA. (*Taking her sister's hand*) Let's not talk about this tonight. We can't bring Daniel back.

ANNA. I know.

(*Leo returns, holding two bottles of wine which he puts on the sideboard.*)

SARA. Where's Alex?

LEO. He's coming. (*Pause.*) Did you hear that racket outside? (*Since no reply is forthcoming*) A couple of minutes ago?

FANNY. No we didn't.

LEO. Well, I did. I went out into the street and I saw a few people hanging about. When they saw me, they disappeared.

FANNY. There are always a few of them out there.

(ALEX *enters and crosses the room to his wife.*)

(*A siren is heard from the street.*)

ALEXANDER. (*Using the opportunity of the others' attention being diverted, sotto voce to* SARA.) Leo's just suggested . . .

SARA. (*Sotto voce*) Not just now.

ALEXANDER. . . . we should . . .

SARA. (*Loudly*) Not now Alex . . . Not now . . .

SERENA. What's the matter? Why is Alex whispering?

SARA. Nothing.

SERENA. Everybody seems to be so edgy today.

(*Silence.*)

(ANNA *goes off into the drawing room and after a few moments, during which she may be heard lifting the lid of the piano and adjusting the stool,* ANNA *starts to play the first few bars of Schubert's A major sonata. They all listen visibly rapt.*)

(*There is a loud knock on the front door.* ANNA *stops playing and returns to the dining room. They all stop,* ADAM *drops the book on the floor,* SARA *walks to her son, lifts the book, hands it to* ADAM *and protectively embraces her son from behind the chair.*)

FANNY. We don't expect anybody, do we? Leo?

LEO. I certainly don't. Unless . . . I'll go and have a look.

(LEO *leaves the room.* ANNA *and* SARA *resume laying the table, arranging the cutlery.* ALEXANDER *lifts* ADAM *from the chair, sits down and then lowers him onto his knees.* FANNY *goes into the kitchen and returns with a set of wine glasses on a tray, which she puts on the sideboard.*)

(LEO *enters from the hall, shutting the door behind him; they all look at him.*)

LEO. You're not going to guess . . .

FANNY. Leo, it's no time for silly games.

LEO. (*Now opens the door with theatrical flourish*) Please come in.

(MARIA *enters. They all fall silent and stop in their tracks. She has grown from a teenage girl into a rounded woman. She carries a wicker basket.*)

MARIA. Good evening.

FANNY. (*Trying to overcome her surprise*) Maria. What a surprise!

MARIA. Madam . . .

SARA. We haven't seen you for such a long time.

ANNA. (*Rushes to* MARIA *to give her a hug*) It's lovely to see you.

LEO. We miss you Maria.

MARIA. I'm so sorry, Mr Singer. (*Pause.*) But you know . . . (*Looking at* ADAM.) Little Adam, how he's grown. Hello, Adam.

ALEXANDER. (*Lifting* ADAM *from his knees*) Say hello to Maria. You remember her, don't you?

ADAM. Hello, Maria.

MARIA. My son is only a year younger.

ADAM. What's in your basket, Maria?

SARA. It isn't polite to ask questions like that.

MARIA. Strawberries, Adam. The first of the season from our garden. You like them, don't you? This year we'd so much, we couldn't eat them all. I've also made a lot of jam and bought some for you. (*She removes a large plateful of strawberries and a jar of strawberry jam from the basket and hands them to* FANNY.)

FANNY. Maria it's most kind of you, thank you so much. Sara dear, would you take these in the kitchen?

ADAM. Can I have some strawberries?

FANNY. We've to wash them first. You'll have some after dinner.

ADAM. Can I have it *now*?

SARA. (*Returning from the kitchen, having overheard the conversation through the open kitchen door*) No, Adam not now. Be a good boy.

MARIA. Madam, please forgive me, but I don't have much time. I came . . . (*Pause.*) We want to help.

SARA. What do you mean?

LEO. Come on, Sara, don't pretend you don't know. (*Pause.*) They are going to take away your money and jewellery and . . . Is that right Maria?

MARIA. Yes, Mr Singer.

LEO. And Maria is offering . . .

FANNY. Isn't that dangerous for her? And for her family?

ALEXANDER. Of course, it is.

FANNY. We can't accept . . .

MARIA. But I . . .

LEO. Let the poor girl speak.

MARIA. Thank you Mr Singer. It was my husband's idea. (*Pause.*) Mr Singer, you may remember him.

LEO. Yes, I do.

MARIA. He's been working for more than three years for you. He told me you'd always been looking after your workers. And he said we should help if we can. And we can. (*Pause.*) I want to do it, too.

ADAM. Mummy, what's Maria saying?

SARA. Maria is going to look after the house.

MARIA. I've this basket. No one is going to stop me . . . (*Pause.*) My husband said, you should make a list of things, please and I should sign it. We keep everything for you until you come back.

(*Silence. They all look at* MARIA.)

FANNY. You think we'll come back? (*Pause.*) Maria, do come with me.

(FANNY *leaves, followed by* MARIA.)

ALEXANDER. Do you trust her?

LEO. Yes, I do. There aren't around many people like her these days. (*They all look at* LEO, *surprised.*) And she's worth more than all the jewellery Mother is giving to her. (*He realises his mask has slipped.*) Well, she's quite all right.

(SARA *and* ANNA *now complete arranging the table.*)

ALEXANDER. (*Gives the book back to Adam, opening at a page*) And your favourite animal is?

ADAM. This one.

ALEXANDER. Could you read what's beneath the picture?

ADAM. The giraffe is eating the leaves of a tree. (*Pause.*) Daddy, why has the giraffe such a long neck?

ALEXANDER. To reach the leaves of tall trees. In nature every-thing has a purpose.

SERENA. Are you so sure, Alex?

LEO. (*Opens a bottle of wine, smells the cork*) Kosher or not, it should be a good bottle.

FANNY. (*Enters now from the drawing room, followed by* MARIA.) Maria came to say goodbye. (*She suddenly touches the gold necklace*) I've nearly forgotten this one . . . a present for our twenty-fifth wedding anniversary. (*She unclasps the necklace.*)

SARA. Mother, you can't do this. Not that one.

FANNY. Of course I can. (*She hands the necklace to Maria.*)

MARIA. (*Puts away the necklace at the bottom of her basket*) I'll pray to God for your safe return. I must be going now. Goodbye.

(*Silence. Maria leaves with Fanny who returns immediately.*)

LEO. God . . . Will He listen?

ALEXANDER. Leo!

LEO. Or turn His face away?

(*They all start to move towards the table to sit down. Suddenly Fanny stops in her tracks; looking at the table-cloth with disdain.*)

FANNY. Who laid the table?

SARA. I . . .

ANNA. (*Sensing her mother's disapproval*) . . . and I've helped.

SARA. Why? What's wrong?

FANNY. Can't you see?

SARA AND ANNA. (*In unison*) No.

FANNY. Look again.

SARA. I can't see anything wrong.

FANNY. (*Angry*) It's *the wrong* table-cloth!

(*Silence. They all look at Fanny with amazement.*)

SERENA. Wrong table-cloth? Mother, what's the matter with you?

FANNY. We always have a *special* table-cloth for Passover.

LEO. Mother, does it matter? Does it really matter?

FANNY. (*Emphatic*) Yes, it does.

LEO. It's absolutely ridiculous. I simply can't believe . . .

FANNY. Whether you believe or not: it does . . .

LEO. Now . . .

FANNY. (*Interrupting*) . . . matter.

LEO. . . . that we've to leave everything?

(*Silence. They all look at Fanny.*)

FANNY. (*Slowly*) Yes, it *does* matter. (*Pause.*) More than ever. And particularly now.

SARA. (*Breaking the silence*) Mother, I'm sorry . . .

ALEXANDER. You haven't done anything wrong.

SARA. Alex will you help?

FANNY. (*Walks to the sideboard and produces another table-cloth. She hands it to* SARA.) This is *the one* you should have put on.

(*With exception of* LEO, *they all help the change the table-cloth and rearrange the settings.*)

LEO. Are you happy now?

FANNY. (*ignoring* LEO) We should sit down.

(*They all move to the table and sit down;* FANNY *at the head of table. They leave the chair at the end, opposite* FANNY, *empty.*)

LEO. (*While they are all sitting down*) After all this, what are we eating tonight?

FANNY. Sara managed to get chicken. Not just one . . . two!

ANNA. Sara, you're a star!

SARA. Yesterday morning a kind policeman let me in the market before 9.30 and I managed to get the last plump chicken.

ANNA. Pity there aren't more like him.

SARA. Wait for the surprise. (*Pause.*) Our neighbours, who breed chickens, unexpectedly gave me one with a few Easter eggs.

SERENA. How have you cooked them?

SARA. Pot-roasted with lots of vegetables; I used up everything left in the larder: potatoes, turnips and parsnips . . .

ADAM. (*Once they are all seated*) Grandma, why's nobody sitting in that chair?

FANNY. It's reserved for the prophet Elijah.

ADAM. What's a prophet?

LEO. An old man with a beard who says things no one wants to hear.

FANNY. Leo, can't you be serious. Just for once. A prophet is a man who . . . well, I'm not really sure how to put it. Alex, you're the boy's father.

ALEXANDER. A prophet, Adam, is a wise man who's like a bridge, a link between God and man. God chose the prophets to talk to mankind, to be His messengers. To teach people not only what they shouldn't do, but also what they should. To be good and kind to other people. To help the poor, the sick and the orphaned. (*Pause.*) Uncle Leo is right. They often demand things we find difficult to do.

ADAM. Yes, but why do we keep a chair empty for . . .

SARA. . . . Elijah. He has an important part in the Seder service – even if he isn't actually with us. Later, after dinner we'll pour a glass of wine for him and we'll open the front door, so he can join us as our guest. Of course, he won't stay with us and he won't drink the wine we've poured for him. But he is with us in our thoughts.

FANNY. Adam, do you know what it is we're celebrating tonight?

ADAM. Yes, Grandma. We're celebrating our freedom from Egyptian slavery.

LEO. As if we had anything to celebrate . . .

SERENA. Don't start again, Leo.

LEO. First they took away our rights, then our livelihood, now it's our property and before long our freedom.

SERENA. Can't we just try to forget for one evening what's going on in the outside world? At this rate we're never going to get round to Sara's delicious chickens.

LEO. The trouble, Serena, is that we've been forgetting about the outside world for years! We've ignored each and every warning sign. (*Pause.*) They're coming for us.

ADAM. Who are coming for us, Uncle Leo?

FANNY. Ignore your uncle, Adam. He's exaggerating as usual. There are some bad people who don't like us, but there are also good people, like Maria. (*Turning to her son*) Leo, pull yourself together, will you? (*To* ADAM.) Now, my darling do you know what makes this night different from all the other nights? (*Silence.*) I tell you what. When we get to the four questions, which have to be asked by the youngest person at the table – and that's you my little one – I'm going to help you. We'll read them together, shall we?

LEO. (*Interrupts*) I'd save your breath, Mother. This year we only need to ask one question! (*Pause.*) Is this night to be our last Seder night together? (*Silence. They all look at* LEO.)

FANNY. Are you absolutely hell-bent on ruining the whole evening for us?

LEO. Your head's in the sand Mother. It has been for years. That's why we're in this mess.

FANNY. What could we have done?

LEO. Leave! Escape! Go abroad! While we could. Others did. We had the money. And even when they clamped down on travel, people managed to bribe their way out. (*Pause.*) It's not too late now.

FANNY. What do you mean?

(*Silence.*)

LEO. What I've just said.

SERENA. Are you serious?

LEO. Yes, I am.

(*Silence. They all look at* LEO.)

FANNY. Leo, are you mad?

LEO. (*Looking at* ALEXANDER) Alex? Anything to say?

ALEXANDER. I don't know, Leo. On second thought, it's hopeless. You must know . . .

SARA. What's going on?

ALEXANDER. Leo asked me . . .

SARA. And you didn't tell me . . .

ALEXANDER. I wanted, but I just couldn't.

FANNY. What are you talking about?

SERENA. Leo, you want to escape? (*Pause.*) Now?

ANNA. Leo, so that's what . . .

LEO. Yes, Anna. (*Raising his voice*) Could everybody stop. Let's just forget about it.

ANNA. But where would we have gone?

SERENA. Leo, you're not making sense.

LEO. (*Deflated*) We could have gone to Britain or Sweden. Even America!

SERENA. Oh, yes. And they're just waiting for us there with open arms, aren't they? Be realistic!

FANNY. The fact is, Leo, we didn't want to leave. Our family has lived here for generations. Ever since the seventeenth century. This is our country, our homeland. We're part of this town. We gave jobs to people and made the town a better place to live. Prosperous and civilised.

LEO. Civilised? Well, just show me evidence of civilisation today. Can't you see, Mother? It's all over. No one wants to remember what we've done for the town. It's history. (*Pause.*) And another thing. Time to face the truth, Mother. (*Pause.*) It was you, who didn't want to leave, not father. Father would have gone to the moon, just to please you.

FANNY. You've no idea what your father believed.

LEO. We had our chance and we ignored it. We waited like rabbits in the headlights.

FANNY. I don't understand you, Leo.

LEO. I'm saying Mother, it's time you admitted that we might have made the wrong decision.

FANNY. (*Remains silent, then:*) I don't know. Perhaps, you're right. (*Pause.*) We thought it was only going to be the Jewish refugees, who'd flooded in uninvited from neighbouring countries with their alien customs, in their tens of thousands, most of them not even speaking our language. Working for less money, taking jobs away from the locals, depriving them of their livelihood. *They* were the strangers; the ones, who had no right to be here. We knew *they* had to be deported.

(*The family is shocked. There is a terrible silence before* SARA *speaks up.*)

SARA. Mother, you can't say things like that. Not tonight . . . especially not tonight! It's what Passover's all about.

ALEXANDER. 'You shall not wrong a stranger, nor oppress him, for you were once strangers in the land of Egypt.' (*Pause.*) Exodus 23, I think.

FANNY. (*Suddenly weary*) Oh, I'm not saying we shouldn't have tried to help them. And we did. Of course we did. But we were swamped. They *had* to go.

SARA. (*incredulous*) 'They had to go?' Why? They didn't have to go!

FANNY. Sara, lower your voice, will you?

SARA. I'm sorry, Mother, but you're using exactly the same language about refugees as the Gentiles use about us. (*Pause.*) That we don't belong here. We're alien. We have to go!

ADAM. Where did they go?

LEO. Ah, now there's a good question, young man. As if anyone here cares.

SERENA. Aren't we ever going to start?

FANNY. Wait a minute, Serena. Of course, we care. The mayor gave a public assurance . . .

LEO. Oh, the Mayor . . . He gave a public assurance? Did he? (*Pause.*) Mother, have you been to the Town Hall, lately?

FANNY. No, I've had no reason to go. Why?

LEO. I thought you might have been given one of these. (*He pulls out a leaflet from the pocket of his jacket, and waves*

it around) Our friend, the Mayor has ordered, with immediate effect, that public employees shouldn't be seen with
Jews in public, they shouldn't shake the hands of Jews, and
that Jews are forbidden to go the municipal park or swim-
ming bath, to . . . Shall I continue?

FANNY. (*At a loss now*) You're right Serena. We really should
start. Adam would you pass round the prayer books, please?

(*As* ADAM *goes to the sideboard to pick up a pile of identical
books and starts to distribute them around the table, there is
a loud knocking at the front door.*)

(*They all freeze. It stops. Silence. Then it starts again, only this
time more urgently.*)

FANNY. The bell doesn't work. We'd better open the door.
SARA. I'll go.

(SARA *disappears, all the others remain silent.*)

(SARA *reappears with* THE VISITOR. *He carries the same small
backpack. As he enters with* SARA, *everybody turns towards
him.* LEO *and* ALEXANDER *get to their feet.*)

THE VISITOR. Good evening.
FANNY. (*To Sara, looking at* THE VISITOR *with suspicion*)
Why have you let a stranger in?
SARA. There is an empty place at the table.
FANNY. (*With sudden recognition*) I think I know you. You've
been here before, haven't you?
THE VISITOR. I brought a present for Adam.
ADAM. (*Lifts the silver Kiddush cup from the table*) Is this it?
THE VISITOR. It is.
ADAM. Are you a prophet?
THE VISITOR. Why do you think I am a prophet?
ADAM. Uncle Leo said a prophet is an old man with a beard
who says things other people don't want to hear.
ALEXANDER. Adam, please keep quiet.

SARA. You look tired. Shall I take your bag? Please sit down. (*She disappears with the bag in the kitchen.*)

THE VISITOR. Thank you. (*He takes the empty chair opposite* FANNY *at the end of the table.*)

FANNY. We've just started our Seder service.

THE VISITOR. I did not mean to disturb you.

(SARA *returns, now all are sitting around the table.*)

FANNY. Where have you come from?

THE VISITOR. From the North.

ANNA. From Russia?

THE VISITOR. I travelled from a place it would be better for you never to know.

(*Silence.*)

LEO. Can you say what it's called?

THE VISITOR. Its name is: Oświęcim, although it is better known by another name. It is what they call a concentration camp.

ADAM. What is that?

SARA. (*Stands up and taking* ADAM's *hand makes for the kitchen*) Come on, Adam, I think we'll go and check on the soup. You can taste it for me.

THE VISITOR. It is the place to which they deported all the Jews from other countries, who took refuge in this town.

ALEXANDER. We were told they were to be sent back to their country of origin to work camps. Is that not true?

THE VISITOR. There is work there. That much is true. For the young and the healthy. For those who can work hard. But not for the rest – the old, the weak, the sick and the children. They're not given work.

ANNA. What happens to them?

THE VISITOR. When they arrive, those who can work are directed to the left. Those who cannot are directed to the right.

FANNY. (*Apprehensive*) And what happen to those who can't work?

THE VISITOR. (*Hesitates then he says clearly*) They die.

FANNY. (*Angry*) Why should we believe you?

LEO. Mother, calm down. We should hear what the stranger has got to say.

THE VISITOR. What I have seen is hard to believe. (*Pause.*) I know that. What is happening is difficult to understand because it is beyond understanding.

ALEXANDER. Are you trying to tell us that these people . . . all the refugees who couldn't work, have died?

THE VISITOR. That is what I am telling you. Yes.

ALEXANDER. But that's impossible. There were a couple of thousand from this town alone. Tens of thousands deported from the whole country. Such a huge number couldn't all just die . . . not within such a short time. Children and young people! (*Pause.*) They couldn't.

THE VISITOR. (*Quietly but emphatically*) They did not die. (*Silence.*) They were murdered. (*Silence.*)

ALEXANDER. Murdered? That's impossible. How?

THE VISITOR. They were gassed.

FANNY. That can't be true.

(THE VISITOR *remains silent.*)

SERENA. Your story . . . Your story can't be true . . . it can't be true . . .

ANNA. . . . that the Germans kill women and children and the sick. No, I don't believe it.

LEO. Remember last time he came? (*Pause.*) This time, don't you think we might at least consider that this stranger's story might be actually true?

ALEXANDER. I'm going to get my wife and son.

(*He leaves for the kitchen.*)

ANNA. (*Frightened*) Oh, my God . . . I want to get Susie.

FANNY. (*To* THE VISITOR) Why are you telling us all this now?

THE VISITOR. I came to warn you.

(ALEXANDER *returns with* SARA *and* ADAM.)

ANNA. Why us?

THE VISITOR. I have chosen you.

SERENA. Why?

THE VISITOR. There are some questions to which there can be no answers. (*Pause.*) Try to escape. Romania is kinder to their Jews and the border is not very far. If you get there, you may gain some time. The Red Army is approaching from the East and within a couple of months this town will be liberated.

FANNY. Is there really still time?

LEO. (*to* THE VISITOR) This place . . . this concentration camp . . . you said it is known by another name?

THE VISITOR. It is known by the name of Auschwitz.

LEO. Mother, you've heard what the stranger said. Let's not waste time. Our suitcases are already packed for the ghetto.

FANNY. You're mad, Leo! We would never get away.

SERENA. Shouldn't we try at least?

FANNY. You try. I don't want to hold you back.

SARA. Mother, you must come with us!

FANNY. Must I?

ANNA. You should . . .

FANNY. I want to die here. You just go. Go! (*Pause.*) Wait a minute . . . Leo . . .

LEO. Yes, Mother?

FANNY. I want to give you this . . . (*She pulls a ring off from her finger*) Your father's signet ring. It's too large for me . . . falling off even from my ring finger . . . Just right for you . . . You should have it.

LEO. (*Moved, he kisses* FANNY) Mother, thank you.

FANNY. Now you really must go!

(*Before they could say goodbye, suddenly, there is a loud bang-ing at the front door. They all freeze in silence.* THE VISITOR *disappears into the kitchen.*)

VOICES. (*From outside*) We know you're in there! Open up!

(*Silence.*)

FANNY. They are here. (*Pause.*) I'll let them in.

ALEXANDER. No, I'll do it!

FANNY. No Alexander, no! Thank you, but I must do it. This is still *my* house. (*She calls out as she goes into the hall:*) I'm coming!

(FANNY *reappears followed by three* GENDARMES. *One is a low-ranking officer, evidently in command, carrying a clipboard; he is followed by two young recruits, barely out of their teens.*)

THE OFFICER. Good evening. Are you ready?

LEO. What do you mean? We're just about to start our dinner.

THE OFFICER. Dinner? You can forget your dinner, I'm afraid! (*Pause.*) You're going to be leaving this house tonight.

FANNY. We were told we were going to move to the ghetto next Monday. Today is Friday.

GENDARME 1. Don't you argue with us! Bloody Jewish witch!

THE OFFICER. (*Disapprovingly*) You shut up! (*To* FANNY.) The Mayor's had fresh orders from the Secretary of State. Change of plan. You've to leave the town tonight.

FANNY. But we can't . . .

THE OFFICER. I'm sorry, but you've no choice. Sentiments are running high in the town. People are angry. You might not be safe here.

GENDARME 1. Today's Good Friday. Have you lot forgotten what happened on Good Friday? You killed Jesus Christ, our Saviour.

ALEXANDER. You surely don't believe in that nonsense.

THE OFFICER. I might not, but many people do. And orders are orders. You must leave tonight! You've been told what you can take with you.

LEO. Yes, we know what we can take with us. But we don't know – do we? – what's going to happen to the rest. All this ... (*His anger rises.*) The pictures. The carpets. The family silver. The furniture! The house. (*Pause.*) What's going to happen to all that?

THE OFFICER. I don't know. It isn't my job.

ALEXANDER. Leo, calm down.

FANNY. Officer, my youngest daughter was married to a Christian, the son of a Protestant priest. He died with thousands others fighting on the River Don. The bishop personally appealed to the Secretary of State that his wife and daughter should be exempt. (*To* ANNA.) You've a copy of the letter darling, don't you?

ANNA. Yes, of course.

THE OFFICER. What's her maiden name?

FANNY. Anna Singer.

THE OFFICER. (*Perusing the list on his clipboard*) I'm afraid she's on this list. Together with her daughter.

ANNA. (*Anxiously*) I've got to go home now to be with my daughter. She's ill at home, and my mother-in-law is looking after her.

GENDARME 1. You're going nowhere!

THE OFFICER. (*Ignoring* GENDARME 1) You may go. We'll pick you up later from your house.

ANNA. Thank you, officer. Thank you so much. Mother, I'm sorry I must go.

(*Anna goes into the hall and we hear the front door open and close behind her.*)

THE OFFICER. Right then. Let's see who else we've got here. (*He hands the clipboard to* GENDARME 2) Take this. Tick off the names one by one. (*Turning to* FANNY) We'll start with you, please.

FANNY. Mrs Samuel Singer, born Fanny Cohen.

LEO. Leo Singer.

SERENA. Mrs Joseph Levi, born Serena Singer

ALEXANDER. Alexander Weiss.

SARA. Mrs Alexander Weiss, born Sara Singer. (*To Adam.*) Be a good boy, tell the officer your name.

ADAM. Adam Weiss.

(GENDARME 2 *finishes ticking off the names from the list.*)

THE OFFICER. Is there anyone else here? (*Pointing to the doors in the room*) I can see that door goes into the living room; what about this one?

FANNY. That leads to the kitchen.

THE OFFICER. (*To Gendarme 1*) Go and see whether there's anybody in there. (*To Gendarme 2*) You go and check upstairs. (*The two* GENDARMES *leave the room. To the family who now try to hide their nervousness*) We're bound to search the house. (*To* FANNY) I'm sure you understand.

FANNY. Don't you think Officer, that you might be asking too much of me? You order me out of my house and from the town where our family have lived for centuries. Don't expect understanding from me, too.

THE OFFICER. I'm sorry, Mrs Singer. I didn't make these orders; I just obey them.

GENDARME 1. (*returns*) There's nobody in the kitchen. Only two chickens in a large pot. They smell bloody delicious. Fucking Jews have got food, while the rest of us starve.

ADAM. But there is . . .

ALEXANDER. (*Interrupting deliberately*) No, Adam, there is *not* time to eat the chickens. I'm sorry, son.

THE OFFICER. Strict orders, everybody out of the town by midnight.

GENDARME 2. (*returns*) House is clear. I looked everywhere, including the loft and the cellar.

(*There is a sudden, loud noise from the kitchen. The two* GENDARMES *draw their guns. The family freezes.*)

THE OFFICER. (*To* GENDARME 1) Are you sure you have . . .

(*But before* GENDARME 1 *could enter, the kitchen door opens and* THE VISITOR *enters.*)

THE OFFICER. Who are you?

(THE VISITOR *remains silent.*)

THE OFFICER. (*To* FANNY.) Mrs Singer, who is this man?
FANNY. (*Looking at* LEO, *who remains silent*) We don't know him.
THE OFFICER. Why is he then in your house?
ALEXANDER. He came to warn us . . .
THE OFFICER. To warn you? Of what?
LEO. Perhaps *you* can tell us.
THE OFFICER. (*To the* GENDARMES) Do you know this man?
GENDARME 1. Never seen him in my life.
GENDARME 2. (*Going nearer to* THE VISITOR) Me neither . . . Who are you?
THE VISITOR. I have no name.
THE OFFICER. Everyone has a name. What is yours?

(THE VISITOR *remains silent.*)

THE OFFICER. Mrs Singer, did he tell you?
FANNY. No, he didn't . . .
SARA. We don't know it either . . .
ADAM. I do.

(*They all look at him.*)

ADAM. He's the Prophet.
ALEXANDER AND SARA. (*In unison*) Adam!

ADAM. Uncle Leo, didn't you say . . .

LEO. Yes, Adam. But there are no prophets now . . .

ADAM. But we've left a chair empty for the Prophet . . . Elijah.

SERENA. Adam, but that doesn't mean Prophet Elijah will really come.

GENDARME 1. So we're now having Prophet Elijah . . .

THE OFFICER. Enough of this nonsense. Time is running out. (*Pause.*) Mrs Singer, do you have a telephone?

LEO. Have you forgotten that we had to . . .

THE OFFICER. I wanted to contact the station. Never mind . . . I'll talk instead to one of the gendarmes outside. (*He leaves the room.*)

(*Silence.*)

GENDARME 1. (*Walking towards* THE VISITOR) So you are the Prophet, eh? Answer me! An extra special Jew on Good Friday.

GENDARME 2. How do you know he's a Jew?

GENDARME 1. I just know. You can tell, can't you? (*Pause.*) From their smell. Same as when you get rats in your house.

LEO. (*Losing his temper*) Shut up, you . . .

GENDARME 1. (*Turning to* LEO) What did you say, Jew?

LEO. Shut up, you idiot. Animals like you have no place on earth . . .

(*They all freeze.*)

FANNY. Leo!

GENDARME 1. (*rushes to* LEO *and hits him so hard that he falls to the ground*) We'll see who has no place on earth, Jew.

LEO. (*Stands up, pulls himself together and calmly*) You are a disgrace to your family, if you have one, and a disgrace to mankind but I doubt you belong to it.

(*They all look with disbelief at* LEO *who is now standing totally calm in the centre of the room.*)

FANNY. Come on Leo, just shut up, will you?

GENDARME 1. (*Concentrating his venom on* THE VISITOR) Drop your trousers, Jew! You hear what I said? Drop your trousers! Or do you want me to do it or you? Because if you don't, I'll tear them off your fucking arse! (*He rushes towards* THE VISITOR *but before he can reach him,* THE VISITOR *calmly lowers his trousers.*)

GENDARME 1. (*inspecting* THE VISITOR*'s penis, triumphantly*) See? What did I tell you?! It's cut! Course, he's a bloody Jew! I knew all along. And a nice specimen, too! They say our girls love screwing Jewish boys! Maybe that's why.

GENDARME 1. (*Turning back to* THE VISITOR) Where are your papers? Now, I'm going to ask you for the last time: What's your name?

(*While this is happening* SARA *takes* ADAM *under her wings and turns him away from the sight,* ALEXANDER *tries to prevent* GENDARME 1 *from insulting* THE VISITOR, *but* SARA *intervenes,* FANNY *forces herself to watch and* LEO *embraces* SERENA.)

THE VISITOR. I have no name.

GENDARME 1. You think this is some sort of joke, Jew? (*He hits* THE VISITOR) I'll show you it isn't. It's bloody serious. Don't you try to take the piss out of us! Everybody has a name. What's yours? What is your NAME??

(THE VISITOR *remains silent.*)

(GENDARME 1. *is ready to hit again but he's prevented by:*)

GENDARME 2. Leave him alone. Can't you see he's soft in the head?

THE OFFICER. (*Enters*) What's happening?

THE OFFICER. (*To* GENDARME 1 *pointing at* THE VISITOR)

Take this man to the police station. They're expecting
him. And I don't want any harm to happen to him, you
understand?

(GENDARME 1 *and* THE VISITOR *leave the room. As* THE
VISITOR *passes in front of* ADAM, *he stops for a second and
without saying a word extends his hand over the child's head
as if blessing him. Then he follows* GENDARME 1 *out of the
room.*)

THE OFFICER. (*Turning to* FANNY *and* LEO) You may want
to finish getting your suitcases ready, but don't be long.
(*To the others*) We'll collect the rest of you from your own
houses. Hope you've already packed. You haven't got long,
if you haven't.

(*The whole family goes out to hall.*)

(*Silence.*)

GENDARME 2. Shame to waste all that food, sir.

THE OFFICER. Don't you worry. Once we're out of here,
there'll be others to follow us in, and mark my word, they'll
pick the bones dry within minutes. Can't you hear the noise
in the street?

(*Shouts from the street have been audible intermittently for
some time.*)

(*First* SERENA, *then* ALEXANDER, SARA *and* ADAM *return
from the hall. They all carry overcoats, which they now put
on, revealing in each case a Star of David roughly sewn on.
Finally* FANNY *and* LEO *return, already wearing their overcoats also adorned with Stars of David, and each carrying a
single suitcase. They all pause for a minute, hardly daring to
look at each other.*)

THE OFFICER. Right then. Let's get moving. I suggest we go
out by the back door. Avoid the crowd that way.

FANNY. No, Officer. If you don't mind I wish to leave my house by the front door.

THE OFFICER. I just wanted to spare you . . .

FANNY. I know. But we are *not* criminals. We shall face those people outside and we shall look them in the eye.

(*They go out one by one into the hall in absolute silence. Last to leave is* FANNY. *At the door, she turns for a moment and surveys the room, watched by* THE OFFICER.)

FANNY. It is only a house, after all.

(FANNY *puts down her suitcase, goes to the table, where she blows out the candles and switches the lights off, before returning to her suitcase, picking it up. She walks through the door and out into the hall with* THE OFFICER *behind her.*)

(*From the street the braying of the crowd penetrates the dark, deserted dining room. Then we hear the front door of the house slam shut.*)

EPILOGUE

The same dining room in September 1945. All the furniture has gone: the room is completely bare. The only reminder of the past is the pair of portraits of Samuel and Fanny Singer. The stage is empty. After a while SARA *enters, carrying a small battered suitcase with* ADAM *in tow who has a makeshift bag in his right hand.* SARA *has aged, but is undefeated: she has managed to turn suffering into inner strength. Her dress and light jacket are worn. She stops, visibly shaken by the empty room.*

SARA. (*Looking around*) Is anybody here?

(*The kitchen door open and* MARIA *enters.*)

MARIA. Madam! Adam! You're back. I'm so happy to see you.

(MARIA *hurries towards* SARA *and the two women embrace after a second of hesitation.* ADAM *not knowing what to do, first holds out his hand, but this also turns into an embrace.*)

(*Silence.*)

SARA. (*Scanning the room*) What happened to our home?
MARIA. Where's Mr Weiss?
SARA. (*Matter-of-fact, to control her emotions*) He died ...
MARIA. Died? But he was young.
SARA. ... of starvation.
MARIA. Starvation?
ADAM. We were hungry all the time ...
SARA. He was a heavy smoker and exchanged his bread rations for cigarettes on the black market.
MARIA. Where?
SARA. In Belsen.
MARIA. Belsen?

SARA. A concentration camp in Germany.

MARIA. I'm so sorry. He was so . . .

SARA. Please Maria, say nothing. (*Pause.*) Good you're here.
You've still got the keys from mother?

MARIA. Yes. (*Pause.*) How is she?

SARA. She died. In Strasshof; outside Vienna, on the way to
the camp.

MARIA. Oh God, I don't know what to say. (*She avoids breaking down:*) I get a couple of chairs from the kitchen. You
must be tired. (*She walks towards the kitchen.*)

SARA. (*Looking around*) Where is all our . . .

MARIA. They've taken everything. . . .

SARA. They?

MARIA. People from the town. (*Maria goes into the kitchen
and returns with two chairs.*) Would you like to eat something? I could go to the market. Had I known you were
arriving today . . .

SARA. (*Sits down*) Don't worry Maria, we aren't hungry. We
had some cheese and bread on the train.

ADAM. With pepper and tomatoes. And then peaches.
Mummy, can I go to the garden to see whether the grapes
are ripe?

SARA. Yes, on condition you don't eat any before washing
them. Agreed? Be a good boy.

ADAM. (*Walking into the living room shouts through the open
door:*) Mummy, this room is also empty.

SARA. Never mind, Adam. Bring us some grapes, if they're
ripe.

MARIA. (*Now sitting down, opposite SARA.*) Do you know
what happened to . . .

SARA. Yes. (*Pause.*) I think it's better if we get this over.
(*Pause.*) Anna and Susie died.

MARIA. (*Cries out*) It can't be true.

SARA. It *is*, Maria. And please, don't cry. It upsets me terribly. I can't cry any more. (*Pause.*) And I can't bear if

anyone else does. Sorry, I can't explain. (*She pulls her chair near to* MARIA *to hold her hands.*) We were on the same train, but in different compartments; the three of us and Anna with Susie. Halfway through the journey the train stopped and was divided. The first half in which we travelled arrived in Strasshof. (*Pause.*) The other half was directed to Auschwitz.

MARIA. Auschwitz?

SARA. Yes. They died there.

MARIA. Of what? How?

SARA. They were gassed.

(*Silence.*)

MARIA. Madam, that can't be right.

SARA. Can't it?

MARIA. A child of five? How can God . . .?

SARA. I've asked the same question. (*Pause.*) And still waiting for an answer.

MARIA. It's been confirmed, has it?

SARA. (*Now stands up and starts to pace around the room*) Yes. By the Central Office for Displaced Persons. (*Pause.*) Serena and Leo . . . they seem to have disappeared without trace. Serena was last seen in a work camp in Lower Austria. And Leo, I don't know.

MARIA. Oh, I forgot . . . There is a letter addressed to Mrs Singer. It arrived only yesterday. I'll get it.

(MARIA *disappears in the kitchen and at the same time as she fetches the letter,* ADAM *appears with hands full of branches of grape.*)

ADAM. Mother look! They are all ripe and sweet.

SARA. Didn't I tell you we must wash them first?

ADAM. Mummy, I tasted only one.

SARA. Is that true?

ADAM. Yes, Mummy, yes.

SARA. Why don't you go and wash the grapes in the kitchen. If you ask her nicely, Maria will help.

(MARIA *hands the letter to* SARA, *and holding* ADAM's *hand they leave to the kitchen.*)

MARIA. Come on, Adam.
ADAM. Yes Maria.

(SARA *impatiently tears open the letter, reads it and then replaces it in the envelope, without any sign of emotion.* MARIA *and* ADAM *re-enter;* ADAM *holding a bunch of grapes, eating.*)

ADAM. Mummy would you like . . .
SARA. No Adam, thank you; not just now.
MARIA. Bad news?
SARA. Leo died. Frozen to death. In Austria. On a march.
MARIA. It's . . .
SARA. (*Sitting down*) Maria, please say nothing . . .
MARIA. Shall I leave, Madam?
SARA. No. Please stay. (*Pause.*) In the midst of all this you remind me there was another world before.
ADAM. Mummy, why have all the people died?
SARA. I don't know now darling, but when you get older I'll try to explain. (*Pause.*) Why do not you get some more grapes from the garden for Maria?
ADAM. Yes, Mummy. (ADAM *leaves.*)
SARA. After a while one gets numb. Nothing seems to matter any more. (*Pause.*) Travelling home, in the same compartment, there was a well-dressed woman talking to a man who could have been her husband. Suddenly, she looked up, and having taken a good measure of both Adam and me, she raised her voice: 'These people! More have come back than had been taken away.' (*Pause.*) All the noise stopped. The other passengers turned away, pretending they heard nothing.

MARIA. How awful.

SARA. (*Stands up and paces up and down the room*) I just looked through her, as if she were not there.

MARIA. The hatred . . .

SARA. Yes the hatred. It never stops.

MARIA. Madam, the jewels . . .

SARA. Jewels?

MARIA. You must remember. The jewels your mother gave me. The day . . .

SARA. Yes, of course. The jewels . . .

MARIA. We've got them. With the list, Mrs Singer and I signed. All safe in our house, I promise.

SARA. Maria, you're an angel. (*Pause.*) The day we left . . . It seems such a long time ago . . . (*Pause.*) On that day a stranger came to warn us . . . Too late . . . He was the last before . . . (*Pause.*) And it was the same mysterious man who on his first visit gave a beautiful silver cup to Adam.

MARIA. I do remember him. I just felt . . . I can't explain . . . He came for Adam . . .

SARA. Do you know what happened to him?

ADAM. (*Coming back from the garden with more grapes overhears the conversation*) Are you talking about the Prophet?

SARA. He is *not* a Prophet; only a man.

MARIA. Are you sure?

SARA. Maria, you can't believe . . .

MARIA. It's all very strange.

SARA. What happened to him?

(*Silence.*)

MARIA. I'll never forget that day as long as I live. (*Pause.*) I was in the crowd, I saw your family being taken away. I couldn't stand seeing it, but I couldn't leave. And the Visitor . . . the mob attacked that poor man. (*Pause.*) He was a Jew.

SARA. Adam, do you want to hear . . .

ADAM. Yes, I do.

MARIA. They gave him a swig of wine and then they beat him senseless. They dragged him through the streets, to a little clearing, overlooking the highest point of the road. There stands a large wooden cross.

ADAM. I remember that place. In the summer, we always passed it on our way to go to swim in the river.

MARIA. Yes. And there . . . (*Pause.*) They crucified him. Where peasants would stop to pray on their way home from working in the fields. (*Pause.*) But when the culprits went back the next morning, the body wasn't there. As if the stranger had never existed.

ADAM. But how . . .?

MARIA. The news that someone had been crucified on Good Friday spread like wildfire. People began arriving from further afield, from every part of the countryside. They came in horse carts and on foot, as if they were on a pilgrimage. They wanted to get near to the cross. Everyone pushed and shoved and jostled to reach it. To touch it. At first people blamed the Jews. But there were no Jews left in town. They'd all left on the train by then.

SARA. Yes, we had.

MARIA. Do you want me to stop?

SARA. No, Maria, I think you should finish the story.

ADAM. Please Maria, go on.

MARIA. Rumours started immediately. People said the body had been taken off the cross and smuggled away. But who would have come to remove a corpse in the middle of night? (*Pause.*) Eventually, when no one could come up with an explanation, people started to talk of a miracle. That our Lord had come back to be crucified again on Good Friday in our town. But this was the most unlikely explanation of all. The man on the cross had been a homeless Jew with no name . . . or date of birth . . . or papers of any sort. Nothing.

And people kept repeating again and again: How could a
homeless Jew be our Saviour?

(*Silence.*)

SARA. And what happened later?
MARIA. It's now a sight of pilgrimage.
ADAM. Can I see the place?
SARA. Certainly not.

(*There is a knock on the door.*)

SARA. The door's open.
MARIA. Does anybody know you've arrived home?
SARA. Maria, please see who it is.

(MARIA *leaves and returns after a minute.*)

MARIA. Madam . . .
SARA. Yes, Maria?
MARIA. There's a stranger at the door . . .

(*Silence.*)

ADAM. Does he have a beard?
MARIA. Yes. He says . . .
SARA. . . . that he has been here before.
MARIA. Yes.
SARA. Do you recognise him?
MARIA. I think I might have seen him, yes.
SARA. So, what do you think?
MARIA. I don't rightly know, Madam.
SARA. I think we should let him in, Maria. Don't you?

(MARIA *leaves the room. After a while the door opens and*
THE VISITOR *appears. All the lights go down with the exception
of a bright light on* THE VISITOR, *standing in the doorway.*)

BLACKOUT

DISTORTING MIRRORS

CHARACTERS

DR ELSA FALUDI – Psychiatrist and psychoanalyst

ERVIN FALUDI – Elsa's son, a law student

DR GÁBOR BÍRÓ – Consultant neurologist and psychiatrist

DR ZOLTÁN ALMÁSI – Consultant neurologist and local secretary of the Hungarian Workers' Party

KATA LORÁND – A patient

IRENE – a nurse

THE CARETAKER

N.B.
The actor playing KATA *can also play* IRENE *and*
THE CARETAKER

Act 1 takes place in Budapest in March 1953 at the time of Stalin's death, and

Act 2 between October and December 1956 during the Revolution and its immediate aftermath

ACT ONE

Scene One

The living room of a run-down block of flats in the centre of Budapest, on 6 March 1953. The lights from an old-fashioned chandelier illuminate a spacious room with high ceiling. A large double door upstage leads to the hall, the door on the right to the bedroom, and the one on the left to the kitchen. On either side of the double door there are two large bookcases overflowing with books. On the right there is a sofa with a large coffee table and two comfortable armchairs; all in need of upholstering. There are more books piled up on the coffee table. On the wall, above the sofa, there are two wall sconces, and between them two oil paintings. To the left there are four chairs round a small dining table. On one side of the kitchen door there is a small side table with a shelf and a gramophone on top with a pile of records on the shelf. On the other side of the kitchen door there is a small sideboard, which doubles as a drinks cabinet. There are a couple of rugs, quite worn beneath both tables; the larger is under the coffee table. The room gives the impression of having seen better days, yet has maintained more than a touch of elegance.

ELSA is sitting at the 'dining' table, writing some notes and smoking a cigarette. She is an attractive woman in her early-forties, who commands attention whenever she enters a room: not so much with her physical beauty but with the presence she radiates. Her hair is swept back into a chignon and she wears a pleated skirt, a blouse with a bow and a cardigan. The bell rings. She ignores it at first but when it becomes persistent, she stands up, stubs the cigarette out, opens the double door and walks into the hall, where she remains visible.

ELSA. Who is it?
KATA. (*Off, says her name but we cannot make it out.*)

83

ELSA. (*Does not open the door fully but keeps it on the security chain as a precaution*) Excuse me, but Kata, who?

KATA. Loránd. Kata Loránd.

ELSA. Do I know you?

KATA. No, but I've . . .

ELSA. What do you want?

KATA. Help.

ELSA. Help? What sort of help?

KATA. I know your reputation.

ELSA. What are you talking about? Don't waste my time.

KATA. It's a professional matter.

ELSA. I don't deal with professional matters *at home*. Particularly not with strangers. (*Pause.*) If you have a problem come to the hospital to make an appointment. Goodbye. (*She is about to shut the door in the face of the stranger, but before she can:*)

KATA. Please, wait. I beg you. I have an introduction. A referral from someone you know. Please, just take a look. (*She pushes the card into Elsa's hand.*)

ELSA. (*Reads it*) Oh . . .

KATA. Can I come in now, please? It's freezing out here.

ELSA. I've to warn you: I don't practise at home. Do you understand?

KATA. (*Off*) I do, but even so. Please, Dr Faludi . . . please.

ELSA. All right, you'd better come in. I'm getting cold, too.

KATA. (*As she walks into the hall*) Thank you. The weather forecast promised more snow tonight.

ELSA. Did it? Spring isn't far off, but March is always a letdown. Just more winter – with a vengeance. Take your coat off.

(KATA *hands her overcoat and scarf to* ELSA *who hangs them on a coat stand. Now* KATA *enters the living room, followed by* ELSA. KATA *is a young woman in her thirties, nice features, well-dressed but without* ELSA's *style.*)

KATA. What a beautiful room!

ELSA. Well, it is, I suppose. Or rather, it was.

KATA. Have you always lived here?

ELSA. For some time.

KATA. It's so cosy and warm!

ELSA. The central heating's working today. Please, sit down.

KATA. Thank you. Have you heard?

ELSA. (*Sits down*) I don't listen to the news these days. So, Mrs Loránd? What brings you here?

KATA. I need . . . I need help.

ELSA. I've already told you. I don't work at home.

KATA. But . . .

ELSA. Look, if you want an appointment, you can always come to my outpatient clinic in the hospital like the rest of my patients.

KATA. All your patients? Are you . . . are you, an analyst . . . I mean . . . A psychoanalyst?

(*Silence.*)

ELSA. I'm a psychiatrist.

KATA. Yes, but I know . . .

ELSA. You know? You know what?

KATA. Why do you deny it? In the past you had patients and reputation for . . .

ELSA. That was a long time ago.

KATA. So why not now?

(*Silence.*)

ELSA. (*Lights a cigarette*) Are you interrogating me?

KATA. Of course not.

ELSA. Why do you think I should answer your question?

KATA. Sorry if I upset you.

ELSA. You didn't. (*Pause.*) It's all, as you say, in the past. And yes, if you must know. I did try to help people. And not always without success.

KATA. Won't you see me?

ELSA. That chapter is over. Closed.

(*Silence.*)

KATA. I beg you. Please, take me on.

ELSA. No. It's finished. You understand?! Everything's different now.

KATA. I'm sorry.

ELSA. Don't pretend you didn't know that psychoanalysis has been discredited.

KATA. And do you agree?

ELSA. It hardly matters whether I agree or not.

KATA. I'm so sorry, I just wanted to know.

ELSA. Mrs Loránd, can I be plain? The practice of psychoanalysis has been banned. By the Communists. That is a fact.

KATA. But why?

ELSA. The Party didn't approve. It doesn't approve now. Psychoanalysis is an alien ideology. Marx and Freud aren't happy bedfellows. The official line is that psychoanalysis is the private psychology of imperialism. End of story.

KATA. That's ridiculous.

ELSA. Who needs psychoanalysis in our happy society? Therapy is for lost, confused and unhappy people who suffer under capitalism. But here?

KATA. But your reputation . . .

ELSA. My reputation? (*Pause.*) 'Comrade Faludi,' I was told, 'you're a naughty girl. A very naughty girl.'

KATA. Are you a member of the Party?

ELSA. You keep asking questions. But if you must know . . . I'm not, not any more.

KATA. I'm sorry.

ELSA. Stop saying sorry. I don't need your sympathy.

(*The telephone rings.* ELSA *stands up to answer it.*)

ELSA. Yes? Who? (*Pause.*) No, I'm afraid he isn't here. (*Pause.*) I don't know. He never tells me. Yes, I will. Goodbye.

(*She replaces the receiver and sits down in an armchair.*)

KATA. Can I ask one more question?

ELSA. I've just told you . . .

KATA. Just one . . . Please.

ELSA. If you must.

KATA. Are you Jewish?

ELSA. It's none of your business.

KATA. My husband is.

ELSA. Well, good for you.

KATA. I thought that your colleague . . . the one who recommended you to me . . . might also be.

ELSA. No, he isn't.

KATA. I just wondered. There are quite a few of them in this profession.

ELSA. '*Them*'?

KATA. Jews. You don't think I'm anti-Semitic, do you?

ELSA. To be anti-Semitic in Hungary is not a cause for surprise.

KATA. I'm not! I swear . . . My husband . . .

ELSA. Quite. No, don't worry. And yes, there have been quite a few of us in this field. I suppose you could call it an occupational hazard.

KATA. I really didn't mean to upset you.

ELSA. Of course you didn't. There are, after all, rather more of us than people would like. I think you ought to leave.

KATA. Please Dr Faludi, don't send me away. I am desperate. I need help. Would you consider having me as a patient?

(*Silence.*)

ELSA. Would you like coffee?

KATA. That would be lovely. Thank you.

(*Elsa stands up walks into the kitchen, leaving the door open behind her.*)

ELSA. (*Off*) Milk and sugar?
KATA. Yes, please.

(KATA *stands up and walks across to the bookcases to look at the books. She takes one or two at a time from the shelves and leafs through them before returning them and taking another couple.*)

(ELSA *comes back, carrying a tray with a coffee jug, two cups and saucers, a milk jug and a sugar bowl. The tray is silver and the china good quality. She places the tray on the coffee table.*)

ELSA. You're looking at my books?
KATA. I hope, you don't mind.

(ELSA *pours the coffee for the both of them. She does mind and wants to get* KATA *away from the bookcases without making it too obvious.*)

ELSA. Help yourself to milk and sugar.
KATA. (*Still looking at the books*) Sorry, for being nosey. Do you read Freud?
ELSA. Freud? Yes, I used to.
KATA. (*Sits down*) What lovely china! It's an old design. They don't make it any more.
ELSA. (*warming to* KATA) I know. They survived the war. The neighbours hid it together with this silver tray, the pictures and the rest of our stuff. Funny, really . . . the china survived . . . in friendly hands, while people . . .

(*She stops short and they drink their coffee in silence.* ELSA *lights another cigarette.*)

KATA. Delicious coffee.
ELSA. Once in a while I like to have the real thing.

KATA. Would you take me on as one of your patients?

ELSA. No, I wouldn't. *Not* as a patient. But I suppose you could come here, if you *really* wanted. (*Pause.*) Informally, as a sort of friend . . . once or twice . . . for a chat, just so we could try to see what the problem is.

KATA. Oh, thank you, Dr Faludi. You can't imagine how much . . .

ELSA. Just don't talk about it to anyone.

KATA. Of course. How much will . . . ?

ELSA. Let's not discuss money.

KATA. But I must pay you.

ELSA. I've made myself absolutely clear. You will *not* be my patient. You can always buy me a bunch of flowers from time to time. I love flowers! Now, let's get down to business. I mean to our first chat. (*Both laugh.*) Before you go perhaps *I* could ask *you* a couple of questions? You obviously know my colleague. (KATA *nods.*) Are you a medic yourself?

KATA. No, I'm not.

ELSA. What do you do?

KATA. I'm a teacher. I teach history in a secondary school in the Sixth District, not far from the French Embassy.

ELSA. Do you enjoy teaching?

KATA. I like the kids. They're a bright bunch. But I hate what they make me teach.

ELSA. (*Looks at her watch*) Oh, my God! I didn't realise how time flies. We'll have to make a date for next week. Is that all right for you?

KATA. Yes.

ELSA. Same day, same time?

KATA. (*Takes out a small diary from the handbag, which she has kept with her all along, turning its pages*) That's fine. (*She jots down the appointment.*)

ELSA. Tell me, why you think you need help? Just in a couple of sentences . . . like headlines.

KATA. My marriage ... My husband ... He was a member of the Communist Party. He didn't join for the sake of his career. There was no need ... He's a brilliant engineer. That's not just my opinion. All his colleagues were singing his praise. Two years ago, he even got the Kossuth prize ... the highest honour ... For services to the industrialisation of the country.

(*Silence.*)

ELSA. And your marriage?
KATA. We had a very happy marriage ...
ELSA. You *had* ... ?
KATA. One night they came for him. (*Pause.*) The usual ... Knock at the door in the middle of the night. And they took him away to the headquarters of State Protection Authority. And there he was tortured. (*She breaks down.*)
ELSA. (*Puts her hand reassuringly on* KATA*'s*) Carry on ... my dear ... I'm so sorry ... And what happened to him after his arrest?

(*There is a noise from the outside: a key turns in a lock of the front door and seconds later a young man, barely twenty, bursts into the room without bothering to take off his over-coat and scarf. Seeing a stranger, he stops in his tracks. Both women are taken aback by his unexpected appearance.* ELSA *regains her composure first.*)

ELSA. You might have knocked.
ERVIN. I didn't know you have a guest.
ELSA. (*Turning towards* KATA). I'm sorry ... This is my son, Ervin.
ERVIN. Sorry to barge in. (*Walking towards* KATA.) Ervin Faludi.
KATA. (*Stands up*) Kata Loránd.

(*They shake hands.*)

ERVIN. Have we met before?

ELSA. (*Interrupts*) Mrs Loránd came for a chat. (*Pause.*) She's a friend . . . well, the friend of a friend.

KATA. I must be going.

ELSA. See you next week.

KATA. Yes. Same day, same time . . .

ELSA. Yes. If anything crops up in the mean time, just give me a ring. You've got my number?

KATA. No, I don't.

ELSA. Here is my card. (*She fishes out a card from her handbag and gives it to* KATA.)

KATA. (*Takes the card*) Thank you for everything.

ELSA. There is nothing to thank me for.

KATA. (*Turning towards Ervin*) Goodbye. Pleased to meet you.

ERVIN. I'm sorry; we haven't really had time to meet properly. Perhaps next time? Goodbye.

(*Elsa stands up and walks out with Kata into the hall.*)

KATA. (*Off*) Goodbye Dr Faludi.

ELSA. (*Off*) Goodbye, Mrs Loránd.

(*We hear the shutting of the outside door, while Ervin takes off his overcoat and scarf and throws them on the nearest armchair.*)

ERVIN. Mother, you shouldn't . . .

ELSA. Don't you start.

ERVIN. Is she a new . . .

ELSA. What?

ERVIN. Mother, don't pretend. (*Pause.*) I don't like you taking risks. What about if this woman, whatever her name is? Mrs Loránd . . . had been followed? In the past you've been.

ELSA. I know. (*Pause.*) I think they've given up on me.

ERVIN. You think so?

ELSA. There are more important people to keep an eye on now. One can't worry all the time.

ERVIN. (*Interrupting*) Don't you think you should?

ELSA. She needs help. Extraordinary woman. She kept asking question as if *she* were an analyst.

ERVIN. Lots of people need help.

(*Silence.*)

ELSA. You're out a great deal these days.

ERVIN. Am I?

ELSA. Yes. What are you up to?

ERVIN. Don't you worry.

ELSA. I *am* your mother.

ERVIN. Nothing serious. Nothing to worry about, I promise.

ELSA. Your girlfriend rang.

ERVIN. What did she want?

ELSA. She didn't say.

ERVIN. I'll call her back. Have you heard the news?

ELSA. I'm so tired of all the lies.

ERVIN. You mean you haven't heard?

ELSA. No.

ERVIN. You must be the only person in Budapest ... in Hungary ... in the whole wide world ...

ELSA. Why not just tell me?

ERVIN. ... who doesn't know!

ELSA. Before you amaze me with your earth-shattering news ...

ERVIN. I don't believe this!

ELSA. ... perhaps you'd hang up your coat and scarf.

(ERVIN *pulls a face, but obeys and comes straight back into the room.*)

ELSA. Now, just tell me.

ERVIN. Guess!

ELSA. Don't play silly games, Ervin.

ERVIN. Come on . . . Guess. Well?

(*Silence.*)

ELSA. You don't mean . . . ?

ERVIN. Yes, I do.

ELSA. It can't be. (*Pause.*) He's immortal.

ERVIN. No, he isn't . . . Not any more! (*Making a great gesture for the announcement*) Mother! Yosif Vissarionovich . . .

ELSA. You're joking.

ERVIN. No, I'm not. Stalin is dead! A date for history: 6 March 1953.

(ELSA *is speechless.*)

ERVIN. You didn't listen to the radio? Not once all day?

ELSA. No, I haven't.

ERVIN. The whole city's ground to a halt. They've already started hanging out red and black flags. And there's more. You're not going to believe this.

ELSA. I stopped believing a long time ago. Not that anything would surprise me . . .

ERVIN. Mother, people out there are crying in the street, as if they've lost a friend or a member of their own family. It's incredible!

ELSA. That really surprises you? And they banned psychoanalysis! In a country where they wail over the death of a foreign despot. Never mind. We'd better to celebrate. (*She walks to the drinks cabinet and looks at a row of bottles*) There's no bubbly, I'm afraid, but cognac will do, won't it? (*Pause.*) I'll get the glasses. Meanwhile please ring your girlfriend. I don't want her thinking I forgot.

ERVIN. She won't. You would make the best mother-in-law.

ELSA. If you want me to be the best, you've to give me just a little more time to practise!

ERVIN. (*Walks to the telephone and dials a number*) Ildi? It's me. Yes, I know . . . bad line. I can hardly . . . Can you hear me? Yes, yes ... Of course I heard ... Shall we meet later? Yes ... In the Corso Presso ... that place we went last week. Remember? Next to the Law Faculty ... Nine's fine ... Me too ... Bye!

(ELSA *has produced a bottle of cognac from the drinks' cabi-net and two glasses from the kitchen. She pours the cognac out, keeping one glass for herself and handing the other to* ERVIN.)

ELSA. So ... cheers. To a better world!

ERVIN. A better world. (*They both drink.*) Do you think things will get better now?

ELSA. I hope so. But let's face it – it's a razor's edge.

Scene Two

The next morning. ELSA's *office at the hospital. A sparsely furnished room with a large desk, an armchair behind it and a single chair in front. The room has two doors: one upstage leading to a wide corridor; the other to the adjoining seminar room which also has direct access from the corridor. A book-case with medical books and bound volumes of medical jour-nals is against the upstage wall. On the right there is a couch against the wall with a low table and a couple of chairs. On the left there is a filing cabinet and a washbasin with a single towel rail with a towel, hanging above the radiator. In one corner, next to the door leading to the corridor, there is a coat stand with a white coat hanging on it. The only decorations on the wall are a framed print of an unremarkable landscape and a calendar, hanging open at March 1953.*

The telephone is ringing but stops just a few second before ELSA *enters. She removes her gloves, takes off her scarf and coat, and hangs them both on the coat stand in the corner. She hurries to the radiator, places her hands on its top but removes them disappointed. She rubs her hands together, walks to the coat stand and puts the white coat on. She opens the door of the seminar room and takes a look inside. She locks the door and walks to the filing cabinet and takes out the file of a patient. She sits down at the desk, lights a cigarette and starts to read. There is a knock on the door.*

ELSA. Come in.

(GÁBOR BÍRÓ *enters. A man in his early fifties, wearing a white coat, bow tie and glasses. Salt and pepper at the temples, he bears himself with a natural authority, but it is offset by his charm.*)

GÁBOR. Hello, Elsa. You look ravishing.

ELSA. Liar.

GÁBOR. (*Tilting his head towards the door of the seminar room*) Is anybody . . . ?

ELSA. No, I checked. All clear.

GÁBOR. (*Walks towards the door, unlocks it as* ELSA *has done and opens it, looking in*) Just in case . . . (*He walks back and sits down opposite* ELSA.) You heard . . .

ELSA. Cigarette?

GÁBOR. No thanks.

ELSA. Ervin told me. I don't listen to the news these days.

GÁBOR. What do you think?

ELSA. What *should* I think?

GÁBOR. Come on . . . Don't be so . . . so blasé! It's an end of an era. And it may also be a turning point.

ELSA. You think?

GÁBOR. Possibly . . .

ELSA. A new beginning?

GÁBOR. It might be.

ELSA. A new dictator, more likely. Nothing will change.

GÁBOR. I'm not so sure.

ELSA. You've seen the newspaper stands?

GÁBOR. Special editions. All in black.

ELSA. At last some colour!

GÁBOR. The city's come to a standstill.

ELSA. It's bizarre . . .

GÁBOR. As a psychoanalyst you should understand.

ELSA. As an *ex*-psychoanalyst, Gábor dear . . . as an *ex* . . . Do
we know the cause of death? Not that it matters.

GÁBOR. A stroke, apparently. Announced on the radio the
day before . . . A massive stroke – that's how they put it.

ELSA. Lucky to the end.

GÁBOR. What do you mean?

ELSA. No suffering. A five-star death.

GÁBOR. Not so sure.

ELSA. If they could, they'd even cover up his death. Having
an impersonator. Immortality personified . . .

(*They are interrupted by a knock on the door.*)

ELSA. Come in.

(NURSE IRENE *enters, a fresh-faced girl in her twenties.*)

NURSE IRENE. Dr Faludi, could you come to the ward, please?
The new patient . . .

ELSA. I'll be with you. Just give me a couple of minutes.

NURSE IRENE. Thank you, Doctor. I'll see you in the ward.
She leaves.

ELSA. The new nurse. Irene.

GÁBOR. The one who . . .

ELSA. Yes. (*Pause.*) The one who takes notes of what we are
saying rather than the patients . . .

GÁBOR. You've got a new patient?

ELSA. That reminds me . . .

GÁBOR. You didn't tell me.

ELSA. Don't be silly. Why should I tell you?

GÁBOR. I'm your boss.

ELSA. Indeed you are.

GÁBOR. You should have told me, Elsa.

ELSA. Look, Gábor it's a case of depression. (*Pause.*) Do you want to see her?

GÁBOR. Not particularly . . . certainly not today . . .

ELSA. You see . . . making fuss for nothing.

(*Silence.*)

GÁBOR. When can I see *you*?

ELSA. What a silly question.

GÁBOR. Is it?

ELSA. Yes . . .

GÁBOR. Why?

ELSA. I can see you at any time.

GÁBOR. You've got a son, haven't you?

ELSA. That's irrelevant.

GÁBOR. In what way?

ELSA. He's my son, yes. And he's also my friend.

GÁBOR. You've told him?

ELSA. Yes.

GÁBOR. That we're . . .

ELSA. Why shouldn't I? He's twenty-one.

GÁBOR. Was it really necessary?

ELSA. I've no secrets from my son. Well, not many. He's bright enough to guess.

GÁBOR. So, you tell him everything.

ELSA. Yes. More or less.

GÁBOR. And did you ever tell him *precisely* what happened here three years ago?

ELSA. Not 'precisely'. Not everything.

GÁBOR. So Elsa Faludi, you do have secrets.

ELSA. I shall tell him. But not just yet.

GÁBOR. I'm sorry. I didn't want to upset you.

ELSA. You didn't.

GÁBOR. So, when are we going to meet?

ELSA. When are you free?

GÁBOR. Tomorrow night.

ELSA. Sunday? What about your wife?

GÁBOR. She's visiting her mother and taking the children with her. To see their granny.

ELSA. Very convenient . . .

GÁBOR. Don't be so hard on me. You know I want nothing more than to be able to spend more time with you.

ELSA. Tomorrow night, then?

GÁBOR. At seven?

ELSA. Fine. I might even rustle up something for a light supper, but don't bank on it.

GÁBOR. Ervin?

ELSA. Didn't I tell you? He has a new girlfriend. Ildi. Pretty girl and bright too. And he's . . . well, they're head-over-heels. He won't be home before midnight.

GÁBOR. Great. I've been looking forward to it. (*He stands up and walks towards the door.*)

ELSA. Before you go . . .

GÁBOR. Yes?

ELSA. A propos of new patients . . .

GÁBOR. Not that again. I've already forgotten it.

ELSA. I wanted to ask you about someone you sent me.

GÁBOR. I'm sorry?

ELSA. She turned up at my flat.

GÁBOR. Just a minute. I sent someone?

ELSA. Yes, to see me.

GÁBOR. Who?

ELSA. This woman came . . .

GÁBOR. Are you sure? (*Pause.*) What are you talking about?

ELSA. Yesterday . . .

GÁBOR. Elsa, wait a minute. I don't understand. You're saying a woman turned up at *your* flat . . . as a private patient . . . and said I'd sent her?

ELSA. Yes.

GÁBOR. Something is wrong. It simply doesn't add up.

ELSA. Why?

GÁBOR. Look, I wouldn't send anybody, not even my own wife ... I mean ... My own mother without asking you first.

ELSA. That's why ...

GÁBOR. I'm not stupid! I know the danger.

ELSA. ... I was suspicious at first, but ...

GÁBOR. What's her name?

ELSA. Kata, Kata Loránd.

GÁBOR. Her name means absolutely nothing to me.

ELSA. So, you didn't send her?

GÁBOR. No. Obviously not.

(*Silence.*)

ELSA. Then, why did you give her your card?

GÁBOR. What?

ELSA. Your card ...

GÁBOR. I didn't.

ELSA. (*Agitated*) It had your name on it. In black and white.

GÁBOR. Elsa, listen carefully. (*Slowly and emphatically*) I didn't give my card to that woman. Whatever is her name ... Kata Loránd?

ELSA. But it was your card she produced. Believe me, I wasn't hallucinating.

GÁBOR. Unless ... I've got a pack of them in my office desk.

ELSA. Who on earth ... ?

GÁBOR. I don't know. Possibly ...

ELSA. I hope not ... That's all I need. She seemed so genuine.

GÁBOR. You never know these days. You've got to be careful. Precisely because of what happened. They might try again.

ELSA. You may be right. (*Looking at her watch*) I must go. (*She stands up*) I've got a patient waiting.

GÁBOR. See you tomorrow.

ELSA. If I'm not at home . . . You know where to look for me.

GÁBOR. Don't be silly . . . (*He moves towards Elsa as if to kiss her.*)

ELSA. Not here.

(GÁBOR *leaves.* ELSA *stands in the middle of her office, surveying it, then picks up a folder from her desk and leaves without saying a word.*)

(*After a short interval, there is a knock on the door. Silence.* DR ZOLTÁN ALMÁSI *enters. He is a handsome man in his late forties, a man who obviously takes great care of his appearance.*)

ZOLTÁN. Dr Faludi?

(*He walks to the door of the seminar room, unlocks it and, like* ELSA *and* GÁBOR *before him, opens the door to look in*)

ZOLTÁN. Elsa?

(*He shuts and locks the door; walks back to the desk, lifts up some sheets of paper, and after a glance, he replaces them carefully. As he looks up, he notices* ELSA's *scarf hanging on the coat stand; he takes the scarf and buries his face in it,*)

ZOLTÁN. Elsa . . .

(*Then he replaces the scarf and leaves the room.*)

Scene Three

DR ZOLTÁN ALMÁSI's *office. A larger, more comfortable office than* ELSA's, *with a larger desk and more comfortable armchairs. Instead of a small couch there is a large sofa with a small coffee table and two armchairs. A door on the right is open, leading to a small private cloakroom. There is also a*

*bookcase but in addition to medical books, there are leather
bound volumes of the writings of Lenin and Stalin. On the
wall upstage there are portraits of Stalin and Rákosi (Prime
Minister of Hungary and Secretary of the Hungarian Workers'
Party); the former has a diagonal black ribbon over its frame.*
ZOLTÁN *is the washroom where he is adjusting his tie in a
mirror. There is a knock at the door. He hurries out of the
washroom and sits down behind his imposing desk.*

ZOLTÁN. Come in!

ELSA. (*Enters*) Good morning, Comrade Almási.

ZOLTÁN. Good morning, Comrade Faludi.

ELSA. You wanted to see me.

ZOLTÁN. Yes.

ELSA. It sounded rather urgent.

ZOLTÁN. Yes, it is. (*Pause.*) Please, sit down . . . A terrible
tragedy . . . Comrade Stalin . . .

ELSA. (*Sits down, opposite* ZOLTÁN; *uncomfortable*) Oh,
yes . . . It's definitely . . .

ZOLTÁN. We've lost a great leader. (*Waiting for Elsa's response
and when this is not forthcoming*) Perhaps one of the greatest leaders the world has known . . . The greatest . . .

ELSA. Greater than Jesus?

ZOLTÁN. I beg your pardon?

ELSA. Sorry, I just thought . . .

ZOLTÁN. Well, an interesting comparison, if it's somewhat
misguided; to say the least. Still, no need to worry, you're
talking to a friend.

ELSA. Yes. Of course. It's just a flippant thought that Christians
in the world still outnumber Communists, despite 'religion
being the opium of the masses'.

ZOLTÁN. What do you mean?

ELSA. Comrade Stalin was a great world leader. Although
the despicable imperialist propaganda dares to smear his
name. With lies . . .

ZOLTÁN. But we can see through their propaganda, can't we?

ELSA. Of course we can. Who would possibly believe that the collectivisation of agriculture was anything but an overwhelming success; or that the Red Army would have done better at the beginning of the war if Comrade Stalin hadn't got rid of most of its best officers?

ZOLTÁN. Comrade Faludi, can we change the subject?

ELSA. No one in his right mind could possibly believe these lies.

(*Silence.*)

ZOLTÁN. Comrade Faludi, may I call you Elsa?

ELSA. Yes, Comrade Almási.

ZOLTÁN. Please call me Zoltán.

ELSA. Yes, Comrade Almási. Zoltán.

ZOLTÁN. Look Elsa, I want to talk to you today not in my role as the local Secretary of the Hungarian Workers' Party but as a colleague. And, I hope, as a friend . . .

ELSA. Oh . . .

ZOLTÁN. I hope you're prepared to see me as a . . .

ELSA. Friend? (*Pause.*) Well, these things do take time.

ZOLTÁN. May I offer you a coffee?

ELSA. No thank you.

ZOLTÁN. My secretary Agnes brews a very strong espresso. Can't I even tempt you?

(ZOLTÁN *stands up, walks around towards* ELSA *and leans against the desk, next to her.*)

ZOLTÁN. Why don't we sit on the sofa? Less formal and more comfortable.

(ELSA *stands up and as she does,* ZOLTÁN *puts his arm around her waist to guide her to the sofa.* ELSA *gently but firmly removes his arm and sits in one of the armchairs.* ZOLTÁN *sits as near to her as possible.*)

ELSA. Comrade Almási... Sorry, Zoltán... Why did you want to see me? Surely, not to discuss Comrade Stalin's death?

ZOLTÁN. Not really. (*Pause.*) But perhaps this is an opportunity I've been waiting for.

(*Silence.*)

ELSA. Yes?

ZOLTÁN. I want to discuss... I want to talk about your future.

ELSA. My career? Do I have one?

ZOLTÁN. Yes, Elsa, your career, your future. (*He stands up, walks to the filing cabinet, unlocks it, pulls out a thick file and puts on the table.*)

ELSA. Future? I've a past. (*Pause.*) As you know.

ZOLTÁN. Yes, I do.

ELSA. Is there any point to delve into the past?

ZOLTÁN. Perhaps there is. (*Pause.*) You know what this is? (*He holds up the file.*)

ELSA. May I guess? It's my file.

ZOLTÁN. Your *professional* file.

ELSA. Of course. The other one isn't held in your office, is it?

ZOLTÁN. Can we concentrate now on this one? During the last couple of weeks I've looked up some of your past cases.

ELSA. Have you?

ZOLTÁN. Yes. Believe it or not.

ELSA. And?

ZOLTÁN. You know it's not my field, but ...

ELSA. Yes?

ZOLTÁN. ... but it was obvious even for me that you'd had some marvellous results. If you could continue ...

ELSA. But I can't. And you know precisely why. I've tried to help patients ... Psychotic patients ... Seriously disturbed patients. I attempted to introduce methods no one had used before. I've tried to reach deep into myself to find a bridge, which might lead to their torment. It seemed to be the only way to understand their fragmented, distorted worlds, set loose from reality. It was a new way of treating patients. I was experimenting, you might say, to chart unknown territories.

ZOLTÁN. I know, Elsa. You had an international reputation. I haven't forgotten.

ELSA. Haven't you?

ZOLTÁN. It's you who has forgotten.

ELSA. What, if I may ask?

ZOLTÁN. The international conferences . . . Without *my* permission, you wouldn't have been able . . .

ELSA. Sorry. Yes, of course. I do remember. (*Pause.*) But don't you think it's degrading to ask for permission to go to a scientific conference to tell the world about our work?

ZOLTÁN. I know.

ELSA. And while we're talking about the past . . . I also pioneered more humane forms of treatment . . . No more electroconvulsive therapy . . . No insulin shock . . . No straitjackets . . .

ZOLTÁN. I know.

ELSA. And look at me now . . . The consequences of that little intermezzo . . .

ZOLTÁN. Yes . . .

ELSA. . . . three years ago.

ZOLTÁN. Can't you just forget?

ELSA. How can I?

ZOLTÁN. Things are changing. Can't you see?

ELSA. No, I can't.

ZOLTÁN. Are you sure?

ELSA. Well, not from where I stand.

ZOLTÁN. Perhaps, I could help, if you . . .

(*The telephone rings.*)

ZOLTÁN. (*Rushes to the phone*) Excuse me. (*Lifts the receiver*)
Yes, Comrade Levai. Yes, it's me. I understand ... Yes,
I'll tell all the members ... Yes ... we're going to hold a
meeting ... Spontaneous ... yes, of course ... as usual.
There's already ... Yes, Comrade Levai, I'll get on with it
straight away ... Sure, it'll be done ... Yes ... Thank you,
Comrade ... Goodbye.

(ZOLTÁN *replaces the receiver, walks back to the sofa and,
before he sits down, he places his hand on* ELSA's *shoulder.*)

ZOLTÁN. The Party Secretary for the District.

ELSA. Anything that will affect us?

ZOLTÁN. It's now official. The funeral is to be held on Monday.
For five minutes everything will come to a complete halt.

ELSA. The theatres and cinemas are already closed.

ZOLTÁN. Every siren all over the whole country will sound
for three minutes: factories, fire engines, ambulances,
boats. There's going to be the biggest march Budapest has
ever seen, passing in front of Comrade Stalin's statue.

ELSA. Oh, yes ...

ZOLTÁN. Can we carry on?

ELSA. Why not? You were saying ...

ZOLTÁN. I can help you, Elsa. (*He takes* ELSA's *hand in both
of his. She withdraws it.*) I want to help.

ELSA. I don't need your help.

ZOLTÁN. You shouldn't be a registrar.

ELSA. Shouldn't I?

ZOLTÁN. We could reinstate you as consultant.

ELSA. We?

ZOLTÁN. I. (*Pause.*) I could suggest, no, tell ... even order, if
necessary the Director of the Institute. I'd have the support
of the local committee of the Party.

ELSA. (*Stands up*) I don't think that's necessary. (*Pause.*)
After everything that's happened.

ZOLTÁN. We could review your case.

ELSA. You think it would help?

ZOLTÁN. Yes. I do. Time has come. We've known each other
for such a long time. How many years? (*He stands up*) Elsa,
I . . . (*He makes a clumsy attempt to embrace and tries to
kiss Elsa but she breaks away, leaving them both acutely
embarrassed.*)

ELSA. Zoltán!

(*Silence.*)

ZOLTÁN. Don't make everything so difficult.

ELSA. You're married.

ZOLTÁN. And so is Gábor.

ELSA. Oh, you know . . .

ZOLTÁN. (*Changing tone*) Yes, Comrade Faludi. We know.
We know a great deal more than you realise.

ELSA. I have no illusions any more.

ZOLTÁN. Don't you?

ELSA. Illusions? I gave them up a long time ago. Shouldn't
we face reality?

ZOLTÁN. But not your determination to carry on . . .

ELSA. With?

ZOLTÁN. . . . with your practice. Treating patients privately.

ELSA. How do you know?

ZOLTÁN. I told you already.

ELSA. Nonsense.

ZOLTÁN. Is it?

(*Silence.*)

ELSA. Yes.

ZOLTÁN. Nonsense . . . eh?

ELSA. I'm a psychiatrist. As you well know.

ZOLTÁN. But you're also ... well, you just described it with great eloquence, did you not?

ELSA. Yes, I was.

ZOLTÁN. You still are.

ELSA. No longer.

ZOLTÁN. Really?

ELSA. Why don't you just say what you want to say?

ZOLTÁN. Does the name Kata Loránd mean anything?

(*Silence.*)

ELSA. Yes.

ZOLTÁN. And what does she ... ?

ELSA. It was you who sent her?

ZOLTÁN. Yes.

ELSA. She's a sort of *agent provocateur?*

ZOLTÁN. No. On this account you're getting me wrong.

ELSA. Am I?

ZOLTÁN. She needs help. She genuinely needs help. Your help.

ELSA. Why don't *you* help her?

ZOLTÁN. I'm a neurologist.

ELSA. And you stole Dr Bíró's card so as to trap me?

ZOLTÁN. I didn't.

ELSA. How did this woman get the card?

ZOLTÁN. It wasn't me.

ELSA. Who then?

ZOLTÁN. My secretary.

ELSA. Ah! It's all the same.

ZOLTÁN. Would you have taken her on, had it been me, who recommended her?

ELSA. Certainly not.

ZOLTÁN. She's *not* an *agent provocateur.* I give you my word. I promise.

ELSA. Why should I believe you?

ZOLTÁN. I swear. She's a close friend of my wife. And her husband was . . .

ELSA. You actually knew her husband?

ZOLTÁN. Yes.

ELSA. Did you?

ZOLTÁN. Yes! How many times must I tell you? He was a friend.

ELSA. And you let him . . . ?

ZOLTÁN. It was thought that he might have been led astray and betrayed the ideals of the Party.

ELSA. So let me get this straight. You believed . . .

ZOLTÁN. Yes . . .

ELSA. . . . that he's strayed from the shining path of Marxism-Leninism?

ZOLTÁN. Elsa, you're going to have to learn to watch your tongue! I don't mind your rather inappropriate ironic comments but others might.

ELSA. Is that a friendly advice or an official warning from the Party secretary?

ZOLTÁN. Don't be flippant. I'm sorry for them. There was nothing I could do.

ELSA. You couldn't . . .

(*Silence.*)

ZOLTÁN. So what are you going to do about Kata?

ELSA. Do you really want to know?

ZOLTÁN. Yes, I do.

ELSA. I've arranged to see her next week.

ZOLTÁN. Good.

ELSA. Informally. Not as a patient.

ZOLTÁN. Of course.

ELSA. Then, I'll decide.

ZOLTÁN. I'm grateful to you.

ELSA. Don't be. I don't think the Party would approve of what you're doing.

ZOLTÁN. This must remain strictly between you and me.

ELSA. Gábor knows.

ZOLTÁN. Oh . . .

ELSA. I accused him of sending Kata.

ZOLTÁN. Yes . . . But . . .

ELSA. You needn't worry. He isn't going to report you.

ZOLTÁN. I hope not.

ELSA. You can rest assured.

ZOLTÁN. Thank you.

ELSA. (*Stands up*) I must go.

ZOLTÁN. Please, don't . . . not yet.

ELSA. Why did you stage this little charade?

ZOLTÁN. (*Stands up and moves close to Elsa*) I . . . I wanted to help Kata. You must believe me. And I felt guilty. No, not guilty . . . Impotent . . . Not being able to help.

ELSA. Perhaps you should have come with her.

ZOLTÁN. And I also thought I might . . . (*Pause while he summons his courage.*) Elsa, I . . .

(*Silence. This time* ZOLTÁN *stands paralysed in front of* ELSA *for a few seconds, then he lifts up his arms to embrace her but when he sees that* ELSA *is again taking a step back, he lowers his arms, defeated.*)

ELSA. Zoltán, I'm sorry. I do have to go. (*She walks towards the door and turns back to look at Zoltán before opening it.*)

ZOLTÁN. Elsa!

(ELSA *opens the door and shuts it behind her.* ZOLTÁN *rushes after her and opens the door. We hear* ELSA's *footsteps echoing in the corridor.*)

(*The footsteps die away.* ZOLTÁN *comes back into the office, shuts the door behind him, and sinks into his armchair behind his desk.*)

Scene Four

Next day, Sunday, 8 March 1953. ELSA*'s living room. The table is laid and a single candle is an attempt to give a festive air to the dinner. There is an opened bottle of wine.* ELSA *and* GÁBOR *are sitting at the table, eating.*

ELSA. Are you going to the demonstration tomorrow?

GÁBOR. What a question! Of course, I am. Everybody has to go.

ELSA. I thought I might not.

GÁBOR. It would be a bad mistake. You *must* come.

ELSA. If you say so.

GÁBOR. You should know better.

ELSA. Do you think that Comrade Almási will order a headcount?

GÁBOR. I don't know. But whatever happens, they mustn't be given any ammunition against you. Especially not by you.

ELSA. Thank you for that.

GÁBOR. You must know the dice is loaded.

ELSA. Yes, I know. I'd love to see my personal file. Must be weighing a tonne.

GÁBOR. Probably better not . . .

ELSA. You think?

GÁBOR. I suppose one day, you might.

ELSA. It's hardly likely, is it? Not in my lifetime.

GÁBOR. (*reaches across the table and places his hand on* ELSA*'s*) Don't be so pessimistic. Have you been listening to the BBC?

ELSA. Why?

GÁBOR. They're talking of someone most of us have never heard of. One of those difficult Russian names . . . Khrushchev, Nikita Khrushchev.

ELSA. So?

GÁBOR. Maybe he's the man of the future. Who knows? Once

there is an opening, a little crack, the whole artificial edifice
may crumble one day.

ELSA. One day? And how long do we have to wait?

GÁBOR. You'll see. It can't go on like this.

ELSA. Gábor, I envy your optimism. A little more? I promised Ervin I'd leave him some. He always seems to be rav-
enous these days. Breast or thigh?

GÁBOR. Is that the hostess asking? Or the psychoanalyst?

ELSA. Come on . . . You can do better than that.

GÁBOR. I don't mind. Both are delicious. Please. More wine?

ELSA. (*Helps* GÁBOR *to a piece of chicken from the china
tureen*) Half a glass . . . please.

(GÁBOR *pours wine into* ELSA's *glass.*)

ELSA. Thank you.

(*They continue eating and drinking. The telephone rings.*)

ELSA. Bloody nuisance. It might be Ervin. (*She stands up and
answers the phone.*) Hello . . . Oh, what a surprise . . . No,
not at all . . . There is no need . . . No, not at all . . . Yes, I'm
coming tomorrow . . . Of course . . . Goodbye!

GÁBOR. Not Ervin, obviously.

ELSA. It was Comrade Almási.

GÁBOR. How does he have your number?

ELSA. Why are you surprised?

GÁBOR. Does he ring you at home?

ELSA. This is the first time.

GÁBOR. What did he want?

ELSA. Just asking whether I was going to the march
tomorrow?

GÁBOR. Is that all?

ELSA. Yes.

GÁBOR. How considerate!

ELSA. There is no dessert, I'm afraid. Coffee? (*She leaves to
the kitchen.*)

GÁBOR. Yes, please. The usual. (*He pours the remaining wine into his glass and upending the bottle he drains the last drops out of the bottle.*) I wish we had more wine. Can I help?

ELSA. (*Off*) No, just leave everything. (*She comes back with a tray bearing two coffee cups and saucers and puts it down on the coffee table.*) Why don't we sit on the sofa?

(*They start to drink their coffee.*)

GÁBOR. Almási . . . ringing you on a Sunday . . . A bit out of character, I'd say.

ELSA. Are you jealous?

GÁBOR. Should I be?

ELSA. He says he feels guilty.

GÁBOR. About what?

ELSA. I don't know. A lot of different things.

GÁBOR. Do you think he's a true Communist? For real and not just for . . .

ELSA. Yes, I do. (*Pause.*) And I have good reason to believe him.

(*Silence.*)

GÁBOR. Why?

ELSA. You really want to know?

GÁBOR. Yes.

ELSA. Because I was once.

GÁBOR. When?

ELSA. After the war.

(*Silence.*)

GÁBOR. You never told me.

ELSA. I thought you knew.

(*Silence.*)

ELSA. Almási feels guilty about not having helped a particular

friend of his. He told me in so many words and I got the
feeling he meant it.

GÁBOR. Almási?

ELSA. Yes. And I'll tell you something else. I think he also
feels he's let me down three years ago. When he might
have . . .

GÁBOR. You've changed your tune.

ELSA. Maybe . . . I have always thought there was more to
him than just the party.

GÁBOR. And what exactly does he want?

ELSA. In what way?

GÁBOR. From you.

ELSA. Shall I really tell you?

GÁBOR. Yes.

(*Silence.*)

ELSA. He wants sex.

GÁBOR. What?

ELSA. You heard. He wants to bed me.

(*Silence.*)

GÁBOR. You're joking.

ELSA. Am I so unattractive?

GÁBOR. But he's . . .

ELSA. So are you.

GÁBOR. That's not the point. He's a Party functionary. He
has to . . .

ELSA. Who's being naïve now?

GÁBOR. And you?

ELSA. Me? Of course I'm not about to be his lover. Upsetting
one applecart is quite enough for me, don't you think?

(*They both stand up and* GÁBOR *is about to take* ELSA *in his
arm when they hear the key turning in the front door and a
second later* ERVIN *enters the room.*)

ERVIN. That smells amazing, Mother. (*Noticing* GÁBOR, *he is surprised.*) Dr Bíró, good evening.

GÁBOR. Hello, Ervin.

ELSA. Whatever happened to Ildi?

ERVIN. She had to go home early. (*Looking around.*) Sorry. Am I interrupting?

GÁBOR. No, not at all. How is the law school going?

ERVIN. It's all right. I just feel . . . I'm beginning to discover what we study is rather different from what's being practised.

GÁBOR. Do you think the law was the right choice? In this country?

ELSA. Odd question to ask now.

GÁBOR. Perhaps. I don't know. Medicine is different.

ERVIN. What do you mean?

GÁBOR. Well . . . Medicine is empirical. And based, at least partly, on science.

ELSA. And therefore it can't be corrupted? Is this what you are saying? Have you forgotten what's happening to psychiatry? How it has been distorted and subjugated to serve . . .

GÁBOR. Yes, Elsa. You're right..

ERVIN. You see, by treating patients, you help . . . Perhaps I can do something as a lawyer to protect people against . . .

GÁBOR. (*Moving toward the hall*) I'm sure you will. I must be going. (*To* ELSA.) See you tomorrow. At the march.

ERVIN. You're going, Mother?

ELSA. Certainly. (*She follows* GÁBOR *into the hall.*) Goodbye.

GÁBOR. (*Off*) Goodbye Elsa. And thank you for the delicious dinner.

ELSA. (*Coming back into the room*) Are you hungry?

ERVIN. Yes, I'm starving. I'm sorry. I didn't know you'd be entertaining.

ELSA. Don't worry. There is some chicken for you. I'll heat it up.

ERVIN. Don't bother, it's still warm.

ELSA. Are you sure? (*She touches the tureen.*) Just about. I'll get a plate and cutlery.

(ELSA *goes into the kitchen and returns with a plate, knife and fork and a napkin.*)

ERVIN. (*Tucks into the food with gusto while* ELSA *sits down opposite her son, watching him.*) Do you like him?

ELSA. Yes, of course. He's been a colleague for donkey's years.

ERVIN. (*Stops eating, looking at his mother.*) Do you love him?

(*Silence.*)

ELSA. What a funny question.

ERVIN. Is it?

ELSA. Why do you ask *now*?

ERVIN. I don't know. Sitting here at the table, eating together . . . Quite intimate, wasn't it?

ELSA. (*Looking straight into* ERVIN's *eyes*) You ask the question . . .

ERVIN. Yes.

ELSA. So, I'll tell you. (*Pause.*) Yes, I do love him. But I'm not in love with him. (*She stands up, walks to her son, runs her fingers through his hair and plants a kiss on his temple.*) I want to clear the table. Will you give me a hand?

(ERVIN *picks up his plate and cutlery and walks with them into the kitchen;* ELSA *removes and folds the table cloth and follows him.* ERVIN *emerges from the kitchen.*)

ERVIN. Are you really going to march tomorrow?

ELSA. Yes. Are you?

ERVIN. I might. Just for fun to see the mass hysteria. I don't understand why you go after what happened.

ELSA. Ervin, let's not start this again. (*Pause.*) I blotted my copy book once.

ERVIN. Was that such a tragedy?

ELSA. Ervin ...

ERVIN. God knows why you joined the Party in the first place ...

ELSA. Ervin ... Will you stop this?

ERVIN. ... a party which promised heaven on earth, equality, freedom ...

ELSA. Ervin!

ERVIN. ... and look what they've done! In a couple of years they've managed to destroy everything, like locusts descending on a field and then flying off leaving nothing but a barren desert behind. They've destroyed or corrupted every democratic institution this country ever had.

ELSA. Of which there weren't many, in the first place.

ERVIN. Freedom of speech, religion, political parties ... Innocent people are tortured and sentenced by kangaroo courts on trumped up charges. The country is run by a clique of potty little dictators who parrot the *ukase* from Moscow: Comrade Rákosi, the most loyal of Comrade Stalin's disciples, has turned this country into one giant prison camp.

ELSA. Ervin, don't lecture me! You know full well how I feel.

ERVIN. But you joined them, Mother. How could you do that? How? Tell me.

(*Silence.*)

ERVIN. Please, I need an answer.

ELSA. It's difficult to understand ...

ERVIN. What do I need to understand?

ELSA. Experience. Loss. Suffering.

(*Silence.*)

ERVIN. Mother?

ELSA. You don't know ... You can't remember everything.

Your father being taken away just when his career as a writer really took off.

ERVIN. You hardly ever talked about what happened.

ELSA. We knew so little. After a while the letters stopped coming. And then the news came.

(*Silence.*)

ELSA. You know the rest. You and I were lucky; we survived in hiding. But hundreds of thousands didn't. When it was all over, I thought we were on the threshold of a new world, free and just. Anything would be better than the past. And that is, Ervin, why . . .

ERVIN. . . . you joined them.

ELSA. Yes. Like so many others, I joined the Communist Party. How foolish and naïve I was.

ERVIN. Do you regret it?

ELSA. Well, there isn't too much point in regretting it, is there? Not unless you can do something. The expulsion from the Party didn't mean much. In a way, I was quite relieved. But when they . . .

ERVIN. Your job?

ELSA. . . . humiliated me in my profession . . . that hurt.

ERVIN. I know.

ELSA. No, you don't. Not all of it. I haven't told you everything. (*Pause.*) Three years ago . . . They submitted me to a 'disciplinary action.' I was threatened.

(*Silence.*)

ELSA. I had to write an official letter in which I renounced everything I believed in professionally. They didn't give me much choice. And that I'll never forget as long as I live. Yes, I know, at least they let me keep my job . . . but not as a consultant . . . as a registrar, a junior member of the department . . . After all those years of being . . . (ELSA *breaks off, no longer prepared to dwell on the past.*) So you see, young man ... I'm still skating on very thin ice. And that is the reason why, whether I want or not, I shall be clearly visible tomorrow, marching with my colleagues, many of whom betrayed me three years ago.

ERVIN. Why didn't you tell me?

ELSA. I was ashamed.

ERVIN. (*Gets to his feet, crosses to his mother and gently pulls her up from the sofa to give her a hug.*) Mother ...

ELSA. Gently, Ervin, gently.

ERVIN. Mother, I've changed my mind.

ELSA. About?

ERVIN. I am *not* going to the march tomorrow.

ACT TWO

Scene One

ELSA's *office. 23 October 1956 (the day of the start of the Uprising): The calendar on the wall shows October 1956. Throughout this scene running footsteps and distant shouting can be heard from the street.*

ELSA is working at her desk by the light of a desk lamp. She lifts the telephone receiver and dials a number. At the other end the phone rings: there is no reply.

She continues writing. After a while she dials again; with the same result. Nervously, she lights a cigarette, stands up and paces around the office. She sits down and carries on writing until there is a knock on the door.

ELSA. Come in.

GÁBOR. (*Enters*) Have you heard what's going on?

ELSA. Of course. Turn on the light, would you?

GÁBOR. (*Switches on the main light*) Aren't you amazed?

ELSA. Not really.

GÁBOR. Come on! Is that all you've got to say?

ELSA. What do you want me to say?

GÁBOR. Don't you think we are in for a shock?

ELSA. (*Stands up*) I don't know. People have had enough.

GÁBOR. It's incredible. Didn't I tell you?

ELSA. What?

GÁBOR. That one day it will happen.

(*Silence.*)

ELSA. I'm worried about Ervin.

GÁBOR. What on earth for? He's . . .

ELSA. You don't know.

GÁBOR. . . . grown up. He's just qualified as a lawyer. With flying colours, I hear.

ELSA. Yes, but he's such a hothead. And latterly he's been going to meetings. Endless meetings.

GÁBOR. Elsa, Ervin is an adult, and not mummy's little boy any longer.

ELSA. I know, but that doesn't stop me worrying.

GÁBOR. He's taking risks. We all are now.

ELSA. Are we? He promised he'd be back from the demonstration by five. It's already . . . (*looking at her watch*) nearly six.

GÁBOR. Elsa, dear, demonstrations don't run to a timetable. Do relax now. (*He crosses to* ELSA *and is about to take her in his arms, when there is a knock on the door.*)

ELSA. (*Moving back towards the desk*) Come in.

ZOLTÁN. (*Enters*) Elsa . . . (*surprised to see* GÁBOR) Oh, you're here.

GÁBOR. Is there a problem, Comrade Almási?

ELSA. Gábor, please . . .

ZOLTÁN. Have you seen the demonstration?

GÁBOR. It's the first time I've seen so many people together who haven't been ordered like herds.

ZOLTÁN. What do you mean?

GÁBOR. What do you think? Those 'spontaneous' mass demonstrations.

ELSA. The crowd is enormous.

GÁBOR. (*facing* ZOLTÁN) Are you frightened, Comrade Almási?

ELSA. Gábor!

ZOLTÁN. Should I be?

(*Silence. The two men face each other, motionless.*)

GÁBOR. Judge for yourself. (*Pause.*) People are angry. They're very angry.

ZOLTÁN. Personally, I don't have any reason to be frightened.

GÁBOR. Don't you?

ZOLTÁN. Are you threatening me?

ELSA. Gentlemen, could you just stop!

GÁBOR. I'll stop. But people in the street might not.

ZOLTÁN. I've known for some time there isn't much love lost between us, but I didn't realise the hatred you have.

ELSA. Stop, please, both of you.

GÁBOR. (*surprised by* ZOLTÁN's *outburst*) I don't . . .

ZOLTÁN. Or is it contempt?

GÁBOR. Contempt? What are you talking about?

ZOLTÁN. You think I haven't noticed? I didn't come from a well-off family. My father wasn't a professor of medicine. I didn't study at a smart private school. I didn't have expensive holidays. My father was a menial worker at the railways. As a child, I never had a new suit, ever, but they were handed down from my elder brothers.

GÁBOR. I'm sorry. I didn't mean . . .

ZOLTÁN. I don't care what you mean. I became a doctor. And you know why?

(*Silence. Both* ELSA *and* GÁBOR *looking at him.*)

ZOLTÁN. Because of the Communists. They gave me chance to study medicine at an age when my contemporaries have been practising for years! Without them I would be working somewhere in a factory.

(*There is an impatient knock on the door, and before* ELSA *can answer,* ERVIN *bursts in.*)

ERVIN. Mother! (*Noticing the two men*) I'm sorry.

ELSA. Thank God, you're here. Where on earth have you been? Why didn't reception ring me?

ERVIN. No one was at the desk.

ZOLTÁN. Where in the hell are they?

GÁBOR. They probably went with the crowds. It's infectious.

ZOLTÁN. Nonsense. This isn't a joke.

ELSA. I don't think you've met my son, Ervin. (*To* ERVIN.) Dr Zoltán Almási, consultant neurologist.

GÁBOR. And secretary of the local Party.

ELSA. You promised . . .

ERVIN. I know I did.

ELSA. . . . to be back by 5.

ERVIN. Things have changed.

ELSA. I've been ringing the flat.

ZOLTÁN. Have you come from the demonstration?

ERVIN. Yes.

ZOLTÁN. They're saying some of the demonstrators are armed? Is that true?

ERVIN. I didn't see any weapons. Not where I was, anyway. The crowd is massive. Tens of thousands, probably more.

ZOLTÁN. You be careful, young man. I must get going. I'll talk to you later, Elsa. Goodbye. (*He leaves without even looking at* GÁBOR.)

GÁBOR. Opportunistic little shit.

ELSA. You're too hard.

GÁBOR. You wait and see. He'll stay sitting on the fence until a spike goes right up his arse.

ELSA. Gábor! Should I quote you on that, I wonder? Put it in your personal file.

GÁBOR. I'm sure that's already overflowing. (*Turning to* ERVIN.) How is your job going?

ERVIN. Didn't my mother tell you? Well, it's fine. Sort of . . . I'm apprentice at the number 6 Lawyers' Co-operative in Pannonia Street.

GÁBOR. In the XIIIth District?

ERVIN. Yes, I've just started last month.

GÁBOR. So not much time to change the world, eh?

ELSA. Gábor, dear, are you getting cynical at your old age? I thought being cynical was my privilege.

ERVIN. Well, the world is unlikely to be changed by the Number 6 Lawyers' Co-operative.

GÁBOR. Perhaps change will happen in the street. Expectation has been building up for a long time. I better take my leave. Goodbye, Ervin.

ERVIN. See you, Dr Bíró.

(GÁBOR *leaves.*)

ERVIN. So, this is where you work?

ELSA. Surely you've been here before?

ERVIN. Never. I came to your old office when I was younger. A bit of a come down, isn't it? Is this where you see your patients?

ELSA. Some of them. I would show you around the ward, but today isn't the best time.

ERVIN. Maybe another day.

ELSA. Yes, it's a deal.

ERVIN. Mother, I'm sorry. I didn't mean to upset you.

ELSA. It's all right. You're here.

ERVIN. I just couldn't get away earlier. What a demonstration! It's like everybody being your friend. You can't imagine the atmosphere. The exuberance . . . the feeling of freedom . . . As though a suffocating poisonous fog has just been lifted.

ELSA. I was worried.

ERVIN. You shouldn't. Sorry for turning up here in your office. Is everything all right? Will it be OK with Almási?

ELSA. Meaning?

ERVIN. He's the Party boss.

ELSA. And you're the protester? I couldn't care less about him, anyhow. I suspect he must have other things on his mind right now.

(*There is more noise outside, the sound of a siren is growing louder as it approaches, and coming to a halt in front of the building.*)

ERVIN. Mother, I wanted . . .

ELSA. Yes?

(*The telephone rings.* ELSA *answers.*)

ELSA. Dr Faludi. (*Increasingly concerned*) Yes... So it's
true... All right, I'll tell him... Yes... Thank you.

(ERVIN *scans his mother's face as she replaces the receiver
and for a moment* ELSA *remains silent as if she needs time for
what she's just been told to sink in. Then looking up straight
at* ERVIN:)

ELSA. It *is* true...
ERVIN. What?
ELSA. Your demonstration... It isn't a peaceful protest, is it?
Shots were fired.
ERVIN. Who said that?
ELSA. Zoltán. (*Pause.*) He's just had a message.
ERVIN. Well, I didn't see any weapons.
ELSA. You may not have. But *they* did. You think they don't
have informers in the crowd? He told me to warn you.
ERVIN. I don't take orders from him.
ELSA. It's just advice.
ERVIN. Look, Mother, I came to tell you...
ELSA. What?
ERVIN.... that I'm not going home.
ELSA. You're *not* going back?
ERVIN. Yes. I am.
ELSA. And where are you going, if I may ask?
ERVIN. To the Headquarters of the Radio.
ELSA. The Headquarters of the Radio?
ERVIN. Yes.
ELSA. What for?
ERVIN. To read out our demands.
ELSA. Your demands?
ERVIN. The declaration... The sixteen points.
ELSA. You think they're just going to give you air time,

inviting you to broadcast your demands on the radio? The radio authorities who have been lying day and night, from the first morning bulletin to closing time?

(*There is a knock on the door. They both freeze for a moment.*)

ELSA. (*doing her best to sound calm*) Come in!
GÁBOR. (*enters*) Did you hear the sirens?
ELSA. Yes.
GÁBOR. They've brought in a couple of people from the demonstration.

(*Silence.* ELSA *and* ERVIN *look at* GÁBOR, *then* ELSA *fixes her gaze on* ERVIN.)

ERVIN. There were a few blows exchanged.
GÁBOR. These are shotgun injuries. They're being treated in the emergency room. I thought you should know.
ELSA. Thank you.

(GÁBOR *leaves. Silence.*)

ELSA. Do you still want to go back?
ERVIN. Yes. I have to. I don't have a choice.
ELSA. Don't you?
ERVIN. No.
ELSA. Well, I can't forbid you, can I?
ERVIN. No.
ELSA. I beg you.
ERVIN. Mother, this is emotional blackmail.
ELSA. I'm just terrified something's going to happen to you.
ERVIN. Don't worry. (*Pause.*) It's a risk I have to take.
ELSA. Ervin, you heard what Gábor said.
ERVIN. Mother, I *have* to go.
ELSA. Why?

(*Silence.*)

ERVIN. Do you remember the story you told me three years
  ago?

(ELSA *remains silent.*)

ERVIN. When you had to renounce . . .
ELSA. Oh, yes . . .
ERVIN. . . . . and you've regretted it ever since.
ELSA. Yes.
ERVIN. If I don't go, I'll regret it for the rest of my life.
ELSA. But, if you do go . . .

(*Silence.*)

ELSA. Ervin?

(*Silence.*)

ELSA. If you must . . . you must.

(*They embrace.*)

ELSA. Come back, safe. Please.

(ERVIN *leaves.* ELSA *remains standing motionless in the centre
of the office, then she walks to the filing cabinet, pulls out a file,
sits down at her desks, lights a cigarette and opens the file.*)

Scene Two

ELSA's *office eleven days later; the evening before the reap-
pearance of Russian tanks on the streets of Budapest.* ELSA *is
sitting at her desk, while* GÁBOR *nervously paces up and down
the office.*

ELSA. After all the fighting this silence is unsettling, don't
  you think?
GÁBOR. Why did you come in? There was no need.

(ELSA *stands up, goes to her desk and rummaging through the top drawer, she triumphantly produces a packet of cigarettes.*)

ELSA. I couldn't stay at home. Do you want one?

GÁBOR. No, thank you. You probably shouldn't, either.

ELSA. I know. This is the last packet anyway.

GÁBOR. With all the shops closed, you've to make it last. (*Pointing to a picture on* ELSA's *desk and looking at it.*)

GÁBOR. Of course, I should have known. You didn't have this here before.

ELSA. No, I didn't.

GÁBOR. Why now?

ELSA. Does it matter? Let's talk about something else. (*Pause.*) I don't know how people are managing. I'm lucky.

GÁBOR. Why?

ELSA. Our caretaker's sister has a vegetable garden up in the hills of Buda and she . . .

GÁBOR. I can't stand that woman!

ELSA. Have you met her?

GÁBOR. Your caretaker? Of course. She always looks at me, as if I had . . .

ELSA. Perhaps she disapproves of our relationship.

GÁBOR. Does she know?

ELSA. She's a caretaker. What do you think?

GÁBOR. Yes. Do you think she's one of the . . .

ELSA. No, I don't. She wants to know what's going on in her fiefdom. She keeps tabs on everyone. But only to satisfy her curiosity. I don't think she's an informer.

GÁBOR. How do you know?

ELSA. My instinct.

GÁBOR. Your instincts? They've never deceived you, have they? (*Pause.*) How is Ervin?

ELSA. He's all right. We had breakfast together. He still believes they're going to change the world.

GÁBOR. And are they?

ELSA. For a few days.

GÁBOR. Everything seems possible.

(*Knock on the door.*)

ELSA. Come in.

NURSE IRENE. (*Enters*) Dr Faludi, sorry to trouble you. I came to see Dr Bíró. They've told me he was in your office.

ELSA. Go ahead.

NURSE IRENE. The patient you've admitted an hour ago . . .

GÁBOR. Yes . . .

NURSE IRENE. . . . he's still in the emergency. He's in coma. He may not survive.

GÁBOR. (*to* IRENE) I'll follow you in a second.

(IRENE *leaves.*)

GÁBOR. I must go.

(*Silence.*)

ELSA. (*takes* GÁBOR*'s hand*) Gábor, what's going to happen? All these young boys . . . And Ervin amongst them . . .

(*Without answering,* GÁBOR *leaves the room.* ELSA *sits at her desk and runs her fingers nervously through her hair.*)

Scene Three

ZOLTÁN*'s office. The same day. The portraits of Rákosi and Stalin have long gone.* ZOLTÁN *nervously paces up and down in his office, looking at his watch from time to time. Someone knocks on the door.*

ZOLTÁN. Come in!

(ELSA *enters.*)

ZOLTÁN. Elsa, how lovely to see you.

ELSA. Have you been down to the emergency?

ZOLTÁN. Why?

ELSA. Gábor was just called. They can hardly cope.

ZOLTÁN. I know. I'm sorry, but I needed to see you.

ELSA. What about?

ZOLTÁN. It's difficult . . . I'm afraid it's about your son.

ELSA. What has he got to do with you?

ZOLTÁN. Nothing to do with me.

(*Silence.*)

ELSA. You frighten me.

(*Silence.*)

ZOLTÁN. When did you see him last? Aren't you concerned?

ELSA. 'Concerned?' Are you joking?

ZOLTÁN. Don't you think at a time like this, he'd be better off at home?

ELSA. Do you have a twenty-three-year-old son?

ZOLTÁN. No, I don't.

ELSA. Do you have children?

(*Silence.*)

ELSA. Why don't you answer?

ZOLTÁN. Yes, we do. (*Pause.*) A girl of ten. With Down's syndrome.

ELSA. Zoltán, I'm so sorry. Do you have other children?

ZOLTÁN. No, we don't. My wife didn't want to. And who can blame her? But we weren't talking about my family.

ELSA. I know. Ervin . . .

ZOLTÁN. Yes, Ervin.

ELSA. A boy brimming with ideals, who thinks . . .

ZOLTÁN. I know, I know . . . But, Elsa, please listen for a moment. Let me ask you something. Do you believe this anarchy in the street can go on for ever?

ELSA. That may be your word for it.

ZOLTÁN. Have you heard what happened at the Party Headquarters?

ELSA. Should I have?

ZOLTÁN. Young conscripts who were ordered to defend the building were murdered in cold blood. They were strung up by their feet from branches of trees in front of the building. I wouldn't have believed it if I hadn't seen the photos. They were mutilated. Innocent boys whose only crime was to be in the wrong place at the wrong time – your son's age.

(*Silence.*)

ELSA. I don't believe you.

ZOLTÁN. Don't you? Then let me tell you something else. I live in an old block of flats. It's very much like yours.

ELSA. How do you know what my . . .

ZOLTÁN. . . . . I went to see where you live. Some time ago . . . It doesn't matter now.

ELSA. Were you spying on me?

ZOLTÁN. I just wanted to see where you live. Is that a crime? The family of one of those soldiers lives in the same block as I do. They called his mother in to break the news to her. When she got home and entered the open staircase, we could all hear her crying and shouting: 'They killed my son . . . they killed my beautiful young son . . .' The lift wasn't working and as she was climbing up the stairs to the fourth floor where they live, she just carried on shouting: 'They killed my son . . . they killed my beautiful young son . . .' until eventually she just ran out of breath.

(*Silence.*)

ELSA. This has nothing to do with my son.

ZOLTÁN. I know. But he would be safer at home.

ELSA. Is he in danger?

ZOLTÁN. He could be.

ELSA. I can't lock him up.

ZOLTÁN. You need to talk to him. Particularly tonight.

ELSA. Why tonight?

ZOLTÁN. Because as we speak, Russian tanks are advancing on Budapest.

ELSA. They're coming back?

ZOLTÁN. Elsa, don't you understand? They never left. They only withdrew. Waiting . . .

ELSA. And now?

ZOLTÁN. They are going to finish the job. There will be bloodshed. Get your son off the street. Before it is too late.

Scene Four

ELSA's *flat, the beginning of November 1956, three days after the Russians entered the capital.*

From time to time distant gunfire can be heard. ELSA *sits in an armchair, reading. The doorbell rings.* ELSA *gets up and goes out into the hall, closing the door of the living room behind her.*

ELSA. (*Off.*) Who is it? (*Barely audible male voice.*) Oh, it's you. Come in. Close the door behind you, it's terribly cold outside. Right, give me your coat . . .

(*The door opens and* ELSA *re-appears, followed by* GÁBOR.)

GÁBOR. Any news of Ervin?

ELSA. Nothing. How did you get here?

GÁBOR. (*Lost his sparkle and authority*) How do you think?

ELSA. Do sit down.

(*They both sit down on the sofa.*)

GÁBOR. I walked and walked.

ELSA. From your flat?

GÁBOR. Yes. I can't believe what I've just seen.

ELSA. Was it your first time out?

GÁBOR. Have you seen the ruins?

ELSA. Yes.

GÁBOR. Whole streets with buildings gutted and reduced to rubble. Worse than after the war.

ELSA. Don't exaggerate.

GÁBOR. I saw a horse . . . on Ulloi Road . . . I don't know how he got there . . . A stallion . . . he was dying . . . he was in pain . . . rocking his head from side to side . . . trying to stand . . . he would get up on to his forelegs, but then he just fell back again and again . . . he couldn't get himself up . . . unable to stand up . . . and he just kept trying . . . over and over again . . .

ELSA. (*places her hand on* GÁBOR's) Gábor, it was only a horse.

GÁBOR. I know . . . but I started to cry and stood there crying . . . in the street . . . loudly . . . uncontrollably . . . my whole body shaking . . . it wasn't just tears streaming from my eyes, it was like as if they were flowing from my very being.

ELSA. My darling, I've never seen you crying. (*She moves towards* GÁBOR *and kisses him.*)

GÁBOR. (*pulling himself together*) Have you listened to the latest news? Radio Free Europe is still encouraging people to fight. Makes me really sick. It's crystal clear that all's lost now.

ELSA. Voice of America is the same.

GÁBOR. Yes, well, the Americans and their awful, endless election . . . Wait until the new President's sworn in . . . As if anything would happen then.

ELSA. Quite. We're off the main stage, anyway. It's all Suez now.

(*Silence.*)

GÁBOR. Oh, my God. I'm so tactless talking about myself when you have . . . When did you last see Ervin?

ELSA. It seems ages. Today is . . .

GÁBOR. Wednesday. The 7th.

ELSA. Four days ago. On the third. I haven't seen him or heard from him since.

GÁBOR. You seem to be pretty calm all things considered.

ELSA. You think so?

(*Silence.*)

GÁBOR. What have you been doing?

ELSA. Oh, this and that. We're strange, you and I.

GÁBOR. What do you mean?

ELSA. You walk in the streets crying because you've seen a dying horse. The day before yesterday, I went out, too. I was looking for Ervin. I knew it was hopeless. But I couldn't bear to stay inside any longer . . . Not for a minute more . . . I was dying inside . . . There was still fighting . . . Did you see it? You'd never forget it until your dying days. The Russian tanks were firing indiscriminately at people, running as fast as they could in the hope of finding refuge in the department store. My caretaker tried to stop me going out, said I was mad. Perhaps I was, but couldn't bear it any longer. The not knowing.

GÁBOR. Oh, Elsa . . . (*He stands up, pulls* ELSA *up from the sofa and embraces her.*)

ELSA. I didn't find him.

GÁBOR. You could have been killed.

ELSA. So what?

GÁBOR. Weren't you frightened?

ELSA. I don't know. All I could think was: I've got to find my son . . . And when I got home, I started to howl. I howled so loudly I thought I'd scare the neighbours. So I went into the bedroom and put my head under a pillow and I carried on until there was no more sound left inside me.

(*Silence.*)

ELSA. By the way how did you get away?

GÁBOR. I told my wife I was going to the Institute. To see what was going on there.

ELSA. And she believed you?

GÁBOR. Yes, she did. In fact, I *did* go to the Institute.

ELSA. Is it still there?

GÁBOR. Yes.

ELSA. That's a shame.

GÁBOR. Why?

ELSA. The Russian tanks might have done us a favour by demolishing it. Dreadful building. Totally unsuited to being a modern hospital.

GÁBOR. Elsa. I came to . . .

ELSA. To ask me to marry you. You forgot you're already married.

GÁBOR. Don't be silly. I came to ask you to come with me.

ELSA. To elope with you? Do I detect a romantic streak rising from the treacherous depth of your subconscious?

GÁBOR. Just stop for a minute, will you?

ELSA. I'm sorry. I shouldn't make fun . . .

GÁBOR. Look, just listen. Please. I've decided to go away.

ELSA. Where?

GÁBOR. Away from here. Away from this country . . .

(*Silence.*)

ELSA. But why?

GÁBOR. Elsa, can't you see it? Can't you see what's going to happen? What's already happening? You, of all people . . . For a foolhardy adventure of freedom . . . Just twelve days of chasing a dream which has turned into a nightmare without an end. The revenge is going to be terrible. Reprisals . . . forced confessions . . . betrayals. I can't face it.

(*Silence.*)

ELSA. What are you proposing to do?

GÁBOR. Escape. Go abroad. With you.

ELSA. Gábor, are you serious?

GÁBOR. Yes, I *am*.

ELSA. Have you considered the consequences?

GÁBOR. Yes. We could travel to the Austrian border – it's still open – and just walk across.

ELSA. Just walk across? And the Austrians are going to be waiting for us with open arms and bouquets of flowers?

GÁBOR. Don't start . . .

ELSA. And anyway, what about your family? Your wife? Your children?

GÁBOR. My wife?

ELSA. Yes, Gábor, your wife. Some time ago, you wouldn't . . .

GÁBOR. Elsa, you must have known. It wasn't a happy marriage. Not for a long time. We stayed together because of the flat and the children. Probably in that order. The children have now grown up. My son's already decided to leave the country whatever happens. He thinks there isn't going to be any future here. And my daughter is going to fly the nest any minute now, too – even if she doesn't know it yet. As for my wife . . . She's just started a new affair . . . She's positively glowing. So, you could say, in a way, I'm free to do as I choose.

ELSA. And you want me to go with you?

GÁBOR. Yes.

ELSA. I can't leave.

GÁBOR. Why?

ELSA. Do you really need to ask?

GÁBOR. Ervin.

ELSA. Yes . . . But that's not all.

(*Silence.*)

ELSA. This is the place where I belong. Despite all that's

happened in my life. Perversely, it is the past which ties me to this country. Without my memories, I would be an empty sheet. Of no interest to anybody. I can't desert my past. To run away would be the ultimate cowardice. And you know Gábor, I may deceive myself, but I feel I was beginning to understand, just a little, how people here think. This uprising, this revolution has made it easier to understand the mentality of these people. Do you think I could learn to read the American, Israeli or French psyche at my age?

GÁBOR. Is it?

ELSA. What do you mean?

GÁBOR. Is it really *your* country? Who's being naïve now?

ELSA. Perhaps I am. I don't know.

GÁBOR. (*angry*) Your country? Was it your country in 1944? Did you understand the minds of those people who lined up the Jews on the Danube quays and shot them? A whole generation of intellectuals, artists and professionals destroyed. Members of your family, your husband . . . Innocent children . . . And you say: this is my country. (*Shouting*) Is it your country, Elsa? Really? Your country! (*Pause.*) Are you mad?

ELSA. Perhaps. But one has to learn to forgive.

GÁBOR. *Forgive*?? How can one forgive evil? Tell me! Tell me, Elsa! How do you forgive evil?

(*Silence.*)

GÁBOR. You know, Elsa this is funny.

ELSA. I can't see anything funny.

GÁBOR. You, of all people . . . you still feel loyalty and patriotism. And here *I* am, every bit Hungarian and Christian through and through.

ELSA. You may be a good Hungarian, whatever that means, but you aren't the best of Catholics.

GÁBOR. What do you mean?

ELSA. Anna Kiss.

(*Silence.*)

ELSA. It doesn't ring a bell?

GÁBOR. Anna Kiss? (*Pause.*) Where did you get this from?

ELSA. What do you think?

GÁBOR. Zoltán?

ELSA. Obvious, isn't it? He wants to poison our relationship.

GÁBOR. The bastard! I should have told you long time ago, but I didn't think it had any relevance to us. I was a medical student. Young and carefree and irresponsible.

ELSA. If nothing else, dear Gábor, they should have taught you two rules at the medical school. One, don't tell patients how long they are going to live since you will be always wrong. And two, don't have sex with night nurses.

GÁBOR. And I did. (*Pause.*) I couldn't marry her. The termination was an unfortunate business.

ELSA. It's a story of the past. It reveals more about Zoltán than about you.

GÁBOR. I envy you.

ELSA. Believe me, there's nothing to envy.

GÁBOR. And I admire you.

ELSA. What for?

GÁBOR. For your strength.

ELSA. I don't have any. I've run out of strength. Can't you see that?

(*Silence.*)

ELSA. Finding Ervin isn't just my sole purpose. It's also my safety net. Without that . . .

GÁBOR. Don't underestimate yourself. Sometimes I think we're all schizophrenic.

ELSA. True. We speak the language of Pavlov but think in Freud.

GÁBOR. No, that's not what I meant. Torn between east and

west, we want to belong to both but in the end we don't belong to either. Elsa, say something.

ELSA. Surely you understand.

GÁBOR. You've got to come with me.

ELSA. I've already told you.

GÁBOR. I love you.

ELSA. I know. I love you, too.

GÁBOR. You're the love of my life.

(*Silence.*)

ELSA. I wish, I could say the same. I love you dearly, but there's only ever been one. (*Pause.*) And that was my husband. You've been part of my life and there'll always be a special place for you. It's just ... It's not necessarily great emotions and shared passions. It's little things, floating impressions of the other which remain with you for the rest of your life. The writing in the sand turns out to be etched in marble. You know, I can still see the way he used to turn the pages of a book. And you turn them differently. I'm sorry.

(*Silence.*)

GÁBOR. I'd better to go. The curfew ...

ELSA. Yes. Hurry or you won't get home in time. Before you do anything, please think it through properly.

GÁBOR. I shall.

ELSA. Ring me once the lines are up again.

GÁBOR. Of course.

(*They walk into the hall.*)

GÁBOR. Goodbye darling.

ELSA. Goodbye.

(ELSA *sees him out and locks the front door behind him. Coming back into the living room, she goes to the drinks cabinet, takes out a bottle, but changes her mind and puts it back. Then slowly she walks to one of the bookcases, runs her fingers along the spines of the books on one of the shelves and selects one at random. Leaning against the bookcase, she starts slowly to turn the pages without really looking at them.)*

Scene Five

Two weeks later. ELSA's *office.*
GÁBOR *sits on the sofa, reading a medical journal.*

ELSA. (*Enters and surprised to find* GÁBOR *there*) Make yourself at home.
GÁBOR. (*Putting down the journal, stands up*) Any news?
ELSA. None. Nothing since one of his colleagues saw him on the day the Russian tanks invaded the city.
GÁBOR. But that was a fortnight ago.
ELSA. I know.
GÁBOR. What can we do?
ELSA. I don't know, Gábor. There's nothing I wouldn't do. The worst part is not knowing what to do. I feel paralysed.
GÁBOR. I wish I could help.
ELSA. I went to our local police station. Or what once was a police station. There aren't policemen any more. Just these so-called volunteers, armed to the teeth. 'Workers' militia,' they're called. Have you come across them? In their quilted anoraks they are a rough-looking bunch. They make the old lot look like members of a gentlemen's club.
GÁBOR. And what did you find?
ELSA. I was lucky they didn't arrest me. They knew nothing of Ervin. If he isn't home by now, they said, he's either dead or has been arrested. Counter-revolutionaries should be hanged, that's all they said.
GÁBOR. Interesting . . .

ELSA. *Interesting*?!

GÁBOR. Yes. Ervin has already been accused of being a 'counter-revolutionary'.

ELSA. What are you talking about?

GÁBOR. Can't you see? The corruption of the language. As we speak, history is being re-written. The national pastime . . .

ELSA. What are you getting at?

GÁBOR. Oh, come on, Elsa! A popular uprising against a system of corrupt, sclerotic despots kept in power by a foreign country is now called '*counter-revolution*'. You remember our talk a fortnight ago in your flat?

ELSA. Yes.

GÁBOR. I've made up mind. I'm leaving. Next week . . . My son's already gone. I got a message via Radio Free Europe. He's arrived safely. The border with Austria is still open. But who can say for how long? Any minute, the gates of the prison might be closed again. Please, Elsa, come with me.

ELSA. How can I?

GÁBOR. What if I waited until we know all's well?

ELSA. Who knows how long that's going to be? I'd never forgive myself if you lost the chance of getting away.

GÁBOR. Elsa, what about if Ervin also wants to leave the country? What future will he have here now? Have you considered this?

ELSA. Yes, I have. But it should be his decision.

GÁBOR. Elsa, I can't wait any longer.

ELSA. You must go.

GÁBOR. Is that your last word?

ELSA. It is, Gábor.

GÁBOR. I don't want to leave you.

ELSA. I know.

GÁBOR. Elsa, please . . .

ELSA. Before you leave, we'll have an evening together. I'll cook for you. At least I can do something. And it prevents me from going mad.

GÁBOR. The last supper?
ELSA. Who knows?

(*There is a knock at the door.*)

ELSA. (*to* GÁBOR). This must be Zoltán. (*Loudly*) Come in.
ZOLTÁN. (*Enters, evidently bursting to deliver the news but when he sees* GÁBOR, *he is deflated*) Ah . . . you're here.
GÁBOR. Our paths seem to be crossing ever so often.
ZOLTÁN. More often than either of us would wish.
GÁBOR. I couldn't agree more. I need to get back to my ward.
ZOLTÁN. Has it reopened?
GÁBOR. Well, in a manner of speaking, it has.

(GÁBOR *leaves.* ZOLTÁN *sits on the sofa and signals to* ELSA *that she should join him. She does so.*)

ZOLTÁN. I've news for you.
ELSA. Ervin?
ZOLTÁN. Yes.
ELSA. What is it?
ZOLTÁN. They found him.
ELSA. Alive?
ZOLTÁN. Yes.
ELSA. Where is he?
ZOLTÁN. I can't tell you.
ELSA. Why?
ZOLTÁN. I gave my word.
ELSA. But why?

(*Silence.*)

ELSA. Zoltán, you're frightening me. Where is he?
ZOLTÁN. At a military location.
ELSA. I don't understand. What has Ervin got to do with military locations?
ZOLTÁN. What do you know about your son's political activity?

(*Silence.*)

ELSA. Very little. I do know he's never been heavily involved in politics until recently. He wasn't a staunch support-er either. But he was hardly alone in feeling our country deserved better. The weeks, leading up to the uprising . . .

ZOLTÁN. . . . If you'll allow me to correct you: 'Counter-revolution.' Just a piece of advice from a friend. (*He puts his hand on* ELSA's *arm as if to emphasise his good inten-tion. She does not react.*) And when did you last see him?

ELSA. The third of November. The day before . . .

ZOLTÁN. . . . The Soviets came to support us.

ELSA. Support? More like an invasion, wasn't it?

ZOLTÁN. Forget about that for now. Do you have any idea where he was going?

ELSA. He didn't say.

ZOLTÁN. Did you ask?

ELSA. Yes. Is this a cross-examination? Can't you just tell me?

ZOLTÁN. (*now ignoring her*) And what did he say?

ELSA. He said he was going to help.

ZOLTÁN. 'Help'? What sort of help?

ELSA. I don't know.

(*Silence.*)

ZOLTÁN. So you saw him on the third. Did you hear any-thing from him after that?

ELSA. No, not directly. One of his fellow students saw him.

ZOLTÁN. Where?

ELSA. In the Ninth District.

ZOLTÁN. Do know you what's been going on there?

(*Silence.*)

ELSA. I didn't know then.

ZOLTÁN. Elsa, I have to tell you that it's serious.

ELSA. What is?

ZOLTÁN. The charges. Your son is more implicated than you
   realise.

ELSA. For God's sake what's his crime supposed to be?

ZOLTÁN. He wasn't just one of a crowd of hot-headed young
   men venting their anger and frustration by demonstrating.
   He was one of the leaders.

ELSA. Leader?

ZOLTÁN. You know about the 16-point declaration?

ELSA. Of course I do. Everyone does.

ZOLTÁN. He was one of its authors.

ELSA. Is that a crime?

ZOLTÁN. It depends.

ELSA. Is it a crime to demand freedom of speech and freedom of opinion? Is it a crime to demand a free press and
   radio? To demand the restoration of national independence? Is it? Because if it is, then you'll be very busy arresting millions of people.

ZOLTÁN. Elsa, please calm down. (*Again he reaches out with
   his hand as if to comfort her, but this time she jumps to
   her feet, facing* ZOLTÁN. *He follows suit and stands.*) You
   don't understand, do you? Ervin was one of their most pas-
   sionately committed leaders. He instigated the inclusion
   of the more controversial demands. And that was just the
   beginning.

ELSA. What else was he doing?

ZOLTÁN. In the Ninth District where the fighting was the
   most savage . . .

ELSA. Why are you telling this?

ZOLTÁN. In the Ninth District where he was spotted . . . yes?
   (ELSA *nods.*) He was fighting.

ELSA. What?

ZOLTÁN. (*Deliberately slow*) Your son was fighting.

ELSA. Fighting?

ZOLTÁN. Yes. (*Pause.*) They had guns.

ELSA. But he doesn't even know how to use a gun.

ZOLTÁN. I'm afraid, he does. Wasn't he conscripted to the Army for six months after university?

ELSA. But he wouldn't hurt anybody.

ZOLTÁN. He did.

(*Silence.*)

ELSA. This is a lie. It has to be.

ZOLTÁN. It isn't.

ELSA. How do you know?

ZOLTÁN. I understand that there's evidence.

ELSA. Like there was evidence about Kata's husband? Is that what you're saying?

ZOLTÁN. Elsa, calm down. I don't know. They didn't tell me.

ELSA. (*Suddenly devoid of all strength, she collapses in an armchair, but almost immediately she pulls herself together*) Where is he now?

ZOLTÁN. (*also sitting down*) I can't tell you. Does it make any difference?

ELSA. Of course, it does.

ZOLTÁN. You can't visit him.

ELSA. Why on earth not?

ZOLTÁN. You just can't.

ELSA. What will happen to him?

(*Silence.*)

ELSA. Why won't you answer?

ZOLTÁN. I don't know what to say.

ELSA. Is it that bad?

(*Zoltán nods.*)

ELSA. Are you saying he's been formally charged?

ZOLTÁN. Yes.

ELSA. So there'll be a trial.

ZOLTÁN. Yes. But . . .

(*Silence.*)

ELSA. Just tell me.

ZOLTÁN. It isn't going to be an ordinary trial.

ELSA. Why?

ZOLTÁN. It's . . .

ELSA. (*Shouting*) Tell me!

ZOLTÁN. . . . It's a sort of military tribunal.

(Silence.)

ELSA. (*Buries her face in her hand.*) Oh, my God. (*Pause. She recovers.*) What can I do? Tell me, Zoltán, what can I do? I'd do anything, anything to save my son.

ZOLTÁN. (*Who has up till now refrained from touching* ELSA, *stands up, walks to* ELSA *and pulls her up from her armchair*) You can't do anything. (*Pause.*) I can try to help. (*He embraces* ELSA.) I will try. I promise. (*Pause.*) I would do anything for you, Elsa . . . Anything. (*He slowly kisses* ELSA *who stands lifelessly in his embrace.*) Anything . . .

Scene Six

ELSA's *office. Early December, 1956.*
ELSA *enters. Shakes the snow off her coat and scarf, and changes into her white coat, rubbing her hands together. She sits down at her desk, opens her handbag, takes out an airmail letter, which she is about to read when there is a knock on the door.*

ELSA. Come in.

KATA. (*Enters with a bouquet of flowers wrapped in paper.*) Dr Faludi . . .

ELSA. What a surprise. Please, do sit down. Coffee?

KATA. (*Sitting down in the armchair.*) No, thank you. I'm in a bit of a hurry.

ELSA. We're not due to see each other until . . . (*She takes a diary from her handbag*) . . . until next Monday. In my flat.

KATA. I came to thank you for all you've done for me.

ELSA. That sounds rather final. And there's no need for thanks.

KATA. Oh, but there is. (*She stands up and hands the bouquet to Elsa.*)

ELSA. (*unwraps the flowers, stands up, goes to the washbasin, fills it with water and puts the flowers in it*) I don't have a vase here. Aren't they beautiful? Thank you so much. Where did you get them at this time of the year?

KATA. The market has just re-opened. Life must go on. So it seems.

ELSA. Such gorgeous colours.

KATA. Dr Faludi . . .

ELSA. Please call me Elsa. Would you?

KATA. Yes, I will. (*Pause.*) I came . . . Is it safe to speak?

ELSA. As much as it is anywhere these days.

KATA. I came . . . to say goodbye.

(*Silence.*)

ELSA. You're not leaving, too?

KATA. Aren't you?

ELSA. No. I'm not. You remember the colleague whose card . . .

KATA. Yes, I do.

ELSA. He's gone. I've just got a letter from him. Where will you go?

KATA. We aren't certain, but my husband is determined. He's had enough. He doesn't want to wait. It's getting more and more difficult to get over the border to Austria. We think it might be easier to slip through Yugoslavia now.

ELSA. Isn't that dangerous?

KATA. Well, there is some risk, but there are guides . . .

ELSA. Guides?

KATA. Well, local people who know the ground and for a nice sum smuggle you across the border. We're leaving at the earliest opportunity.

ELSA. Good luck.

KATA. We may need it. And your son? I should've asked earlier but I'm so preoccupied. Is there any news?

ELSA. Nothing new. Send me a card when you're safely there, will you?

(*They both stand up, start awkwardly to shake hands but end up hugging each other.*)

KATA. Goodbye, Elsa. And thank you again.

ELSA. Goodbye.

(*After* KATA *has left,* ELSA *returns to her desk and continues reading the airmail. There is a knock on the door.*)

ELSA. Come in!

ZOLTÁN. (*Enters*) Elsa darling, where on the earth have you been yesterday?

ELSA. Am I obliged to give an account of every step I take?

ZOLTÁN. I'm worried about you. And with reason.

ELSA. You worry about me. I'm worried about *my son.* Any news?

ZOLTÁN. Yes. And no.

ELSA. Don't play silly games.

ZOLTÁN. The sentence will be passed today.

ELSA. Oh . . .

ZOLTÁN. They're going to call me.

ELSA. Who?

ZOLTÁN. Does it matter who?

ELSA. People in the shadows. The faceless and nameless 'they'.

ZOLTÁN. (*As he passes* ELSA'*s desk, he notices the airmail letter*) From Gábor?

ELSA. Yes.

ZOLTÁN. Do you miss him?

ELSA. (*Looking straight at* ZOLTÁN.) Yes. (*Seeing the effect of her answer.*) I can't lie.

ZOLTÁN. Lies? And what about your little underground practice?

ELSA. Can't you forget about it?

ZOLTÁN. Don't you think we did not know all along? Beside, it must have been pretty obvious when I sent Kata to you.

ELSA. I would keep quiet about Kata. The Party wouldn't approve.

ZOLTÁN. Are you threatening me?

ELSA. Don't be stupid. After my public humiliation I had to do it to restore my self-esteem. You may call it a small act of defiance.

ZOLTÁN. I'm sorry about what happened. How many times do I have to repeat it?

ELSA. Never mind.

ZOLTÁN. How is he?

ELSA. Gábor? You can read his letter if you want.

ZOLTÁN. I don't.

ELSA. Others did.

ZOLTÁN. Meaning?

ELSA. I'm sure you can guess. It was steamed open. They didn't even bother to stick it down properly again.

ZOLTÁN. How is he?

ELSA. He's well. He got through the language exam, and he's preparing for the next hurdle.

ZOLTÁN. In the corridor I bumped into Kata. She shouldn't have come here. What did she want?

ELSA. She came to set up her next appointment. I haven't seen her for some time.

ZOLTÁN. How is she?

ELSA. She'll be all right. She's convinced I've helped her. Zoltán, I want to ask a question.

ZOLTÁN. Yes.

ELSA. You don't believe in psychoanalysis. And yet you sent Kata.

ZOLTÁN. I don't believe in psychoanalysis. But I believed *you*'d be able to help her in whatever way you thought best.

ELSA. Thank you. I appreciate the recognition coming from you. A little too late though, don't you think?

ZOLTÁN. Well, you *have* helped her. Perhaps we should leave it at that?

(*Silence.*)

ELSA. Don't laugh at what I'm going to say. Occasionally I feel we don't live in a real world. Have you ever read Plato?

ZOLTÁN. What an extraordinary question.

ELSA. In the Marxist University you must have.

ZOLTÁN. Yes, but that was some time ago.

ELSA. Come on Comrade. The first year before Scientific Socialism and Marxism and Leninism, there were two semesters of . . .

ZOLTÁN. . . . history of philosophy . . .

ELSA. . . . including Plato.

ZOLTÁN. (*Tries to lighten the conversation*) As in Platonic love?

ELSA. No. As in his treatise, *The Republic.* Does the allegory of the cave ring a bell?

ZOLTÁN. Not really.

ELSA. People are living in a cave chained to the ground, and facing a blank wall. All they can see are shadows. Shadows of people and objects and events. And all this show is projected from behind them onto the wall by the light of a fire. Real life appears to them solely as shadows and they have to try to read meaning into what they see.

ZOLTÁN. And?

ELSA. We *are* those people in the cave. We look at life through a distorting mirror. A two-way mirror. (*Pause.*) Its focus is manipulated by those who are in control over us.

ZOLTÁN. As bad as that?

ELSA. Yes.

ZOLTÁN. Don't you think we are making the future better.

ELSA. Do you believe what you're saying? Zoltán, you're amazing.

ZOLTÁN. Elsa, where were you last night? You didn't answer my question.

ELSA. It's none of your business.

ZOLTÁN. Isn't it?

ELSA. Why?

ZOLTÁN. You certainly weren't at home. I called you.

ELSA. I'm going to surprise you.

ZOLTÁN. Do you think you still can?

ELSA. I think I might.

ZOLTÁN. Try me.

ELSA. I took part in a demonstration.

(*Silence.*)

ZOLTÁN. You didn't surprise me. I did know.

ELSA. They were spying on me?

ZOLTÁN. Never mind. Demonstrations have been banned. All demonstrations. You must know.

ELSA. I do.

ZOLTÁN. Are you mad? They could have . . .

ELSA. But they didn't, you see.

ZOLTÁN. Is this a sort of death wish?

ELSA. Oh, are you embarking on a late career in analysis? I didn't realise.

ZOLTÁN. (*Angry*) This isn't a joke, Elsa.

ELSA. No, it isn't. (*Pause.*) You're right.

ZOLTÁN. So why did you?

ELSA. I didn't plan to go. (*Pause.*) I got caught up.

ZOLTÁN. You don't just get caught up in a demonstration.

ELSA. If you want to know, I left the Institute earlier yesterday and set off on foot on my usual route home. It's
half an hour's brisk walk. I was about to enter our street
when I heard this strange noise. I didn't know what it was.
Quite soft, but relentless. (*Pause.*) Over the last few weeks,
we've been living with noise. Big, dramatic noises: gunfire
and machineguns, explosions from Molotov cocktails and
hand grenades, the thunder of tanks rolling in. (*Pause.*)
But this was altogether different. Somehow more threatening. (*Pause.*) For a minute I stopped. Then I turned, and
hurried back towards the boulevard. I wanted to know.
Suddenly, I saw them. It was a strange sight; something I'd
never seen before. And at first I couldn't work it out what I
was seeing. (*Pause.*) Then I realised. (*Pause.*) They were *all*
women: thousands and thousands of women.

ZOLTÁN. (*Interrupting*) Yes, I know. Apparently some
30,000.

ELSA. (*Ignoring him*) Many wore black. Some were carrying
the national flag with a hole in the middle. The hated coat-
of-arms cut out. It was like an elemental force. As if . . . as
if in a Greek tragedy the chorus was about to take over. Not
just to express the pain of murders committed off-stage,
but to represent fate itself. It seemed totally unreal. And
there wasn't a single man in the crowd. After all what's
been happening earlier: men in demonstrations . . . men
racing through the street . . . men on the barricades . . .
men fighting . . . men killing each other. Now, the only
men in sight were standing on the pavement watching
with disbelief. For a while I've just stood there on the pavement, awe-struck, just watching. And then suddenly, as if
in a daze, I'd started to walk on the pavement. First slowly,
then faster to catch up with them.

ZOLTÁN. Elsa, did you think what you were doing?

ELSA. (*Ignoring* ZOLTÁN). Eventually I stepped off the pavement and I joined them. I couldn't resist. I was swept away by the tide of their emotions, their anger, their dignity and their grief. (*Pause.*) I had to be one of them. (*Turning to Zoltán.*) You know, Zoltán, I've tried to help people to define their personalities . . . to explore their subconscious . . . to confront the shadows of their past. And now I was all too happy to surrender my own identity; just to be one of the crowd. (*Pause.*) And then something inexplicable happened. My anger, my fear and grief flew away into this anonymous, massive tide of sentiment. Marching with those women I felt . . . I felt I could do anything. (*Pause.*) But of course, there was very little we could actually do. Even so, I went home quite elated. A point had been made.

(*Silence.*)

ZOLTÁN. Are you insane? Don't you realise how dangerous it was?

ELSA. It didn't seem to matter at the time. And you know what? It doesn't matter now either. The strength I gained there will remain with me for the rest of my life. When I came in today, subconsciously perhaps I didn't follow my daily routine.

ZOLTÁN. What do you mean?

ELSA. I didn't check whether there was anyone in the seminar room. I didn't care.

ZOLTÁN. I'm happy nothing happened. But please, don't be stupid again. Promise, please.

ELSA. I don't promise anything.

(*The telephone rings.*)

ELSA. (*Rushes to the phone and picks up the receiver.*) Dr Faludi. (*Pause.*) Oh, yes. (*Pause.*) Comrade Almási is here. Zoltán, this is for you.

ZOLTÁN. (*Stands up, to* ELSA.) I asked the switchboard to divert the call. (*Into the receiver:*) Almási.

(*Long pause while* ZOLTÁN *listens.* ELSA *lights another cigarette and starts pacing up and down the office.* ZOLTÁN *does not take off his eyes of her.*)

ZOLTÁN. Yes, I understand. Thank you. Goodbye.

(*He replaces the receiver, walks to* ELSA *and tries to embrace her. She breaks free.*)

ELSA. Zoltán, no! What is the news?

ZOLTÁN. Elsa, please, do sit down. (*He gently ushers her to the sofa, sits next to her and holds her hand.*) I'm desperately sorry. (*Pause.*) I don't know how to tell you . . . They . . .

ELSA. Tell me for God's sake!

ZOLTÁN. They found him guilty.

ELSA. Guilty of what?

ZOLTÁN. Of conspiracy against the People's Republic.

ELSA. (*Realising the gravity of the charge.*) But he . . .

ZOLTÁN. Organising and leading events whose aim was to overturn the existing Socialist order . . .

ELSA. But that's a lie.

ZOLTÁN. . . . in the service of a foreign, imperialist enemy.

ELSA. (*Jumps up from the sofa*) That's crazy! (*Shouting*) What an absurd idea. He wasn't in the service of anybody. Just because he dared to think differently. If he was in the service of anything, it was freedom.

ZOLTÁN. Elsa, I know how you feel.

ELSA. It's a lie, a stupid lie!

ZOLTÁN. (*Walks towards Elsa; he takes her hand and leads her towards the sofa. They both sit down.*) Elsa . . . It isn't. They've got evidence.

ELSA. (*Increasingly frightened, gradually realising what is coming.*) But he couldn't do all that.

ZOLTÁN. Yes, he could.

ELSA. Yes, but . . . Anyone can say . . .

ZOLTÁN. There's additional . . .

ELSA. I don't believe it.

ZOLTÁN. . . . . overwhelming evidence. He used weapons with
intent to kill.

ELSA. But Ervin wouldn't harm anybody.

ZOLTÁN. Elsa, you may not have known your son as well as
you thought you did.

ELSA. (*Sits down in one of the armchairs.*) They found him
guilty?

ZOLTÁN. Yes.

ELSA. When is the sentencing?

ZOLTÁN. It's done.

ELSA. When?

ZOLTÁN. Earlier today.

ELSA. But the trial has only just started.

ZOLTÁN. (*Reaches out to hold* ELSA's *hand but she pulls it
away*) Elsa, you don't seem to understand. (*Pause.*) I've
already told you. It was a military tribunal. A sort of court
martial.

(*Silence.*)

ELSA. What happened?

(*Silence.*)

ZOLTÁN. (*Moving towards* ELSA.) He was sentenced to
death.

ELSA. (*Buries her face in her hands, cries out loud and then
pulls herself together*) When can I see him?

ZOLTÁN. You can't.

ELSA. Why?

ZOLTÁN. Ervin is to be executed. (*Pause.*) This afternoon.

ELSA. (*She nearly breaks down*) They can't kill him. They
can't! Zoltán, you promised . . .

ZOLTÁN. Believe me, I tried.

(ZOLTÁN *suddenly stops, noticing the change in* ELSA*'s expression. There is silence. When* ELSA *speaks, her tone is quite different, almost back in control.*)

ELSA. Yes, I'm sure you did.

ZOLTÁN. I can't do anything more.

ELSA. I know.

ZOLTÁN. (*Stands up to leave, but first tries again to comfort* ELSA *by holding her. Gently she rejects the attempt.*) I'll see you later.

ELSA. Yes.

ZOLTÁN. Can I take you home tonight?

ELSA. I'll find my way.

ZOLTÁN. You have to be careful.

ELSA. I know.

(ZOLTÁN *leaves. Silence.* ELSA *stands up, walks round the desk and, facing the upstage wall, she emits a heart-breaking cry.*)

ZOLTÁN. (*Distressed, re-enters at once, without knocking, having heard her cry*) Elsa, I just can't leave you here.

ELSA. (*Making a supreme effort to hold herself together*) Don't you understand? Just leave me.

ZOLTÁN. Can I come with you?

ELSA. No, you can't. Why don't you go to your friends who killed my son?

ZOLTÁN. Elsa!

(*Silence.*)

ELSA. Goodbye, Zoltán. (*Long pause.*) Looks like more snow tonight.

(*After* ZOLTÁN *leaves,* ELSA *stands for a minute motionless, locks the door, then walks to her desk, sits down and buries her face in her hand, without crying.*)

(*Silence.*)

(*There is a sudden prolonged and violent banging on the door.*)

(ELSA *remains motionless.*)

(*More banging on the door.*)

(ELSA *stands up, walks to the coat stand and puts on her overcoat with the shawl. She unlocks the door.*)

(*The banging stops.*)

ELSA. (*Opens the door and we see the silhouette of two men*) I *am* ready. (*Pause.*) I have been waiting for you.

(*From the door she turns back*)

ELSA. Just a second. Don't worry, I'm not going to escape.

(*She walks to her desk, picks up the photo of her son and puts it into her handbag. Then she walks to the washbasin, gathers* KATA'*s flowers and smells them.*)

ELSA. I can't leave these beautiful flowers here, can I?

BLACKOUT

STOLEN YEARS

CHARACTERS

LÁSZLÓ (LACI)

VERA (LACI's wife)

ROBERT (ROBI)

MARIAN

LÁSZLÓ, ROBERT and MARIAN are all of the same age; in their early fifties, while VERA is a couple of years older. Laci, Robi and Marian were school friends.

Acts One and Two take place in Budapest, in the flat of Laci and Vera on a Sunday, towards the end of September 1989, immediately after Communism collapsed.

ACT ONE

The living room of a middle-class family. The door upstage opens to the entrance hall, the one on the left to the bedroom, and the one on the right to the kitchen. The room is modestly furnished. Towards the kitchen door there is a dining table with four chairs; towards the bedroom a sofa with a coffee table and two small armchairs. On the upstage wall there is one of those combined cupboards and bookcases which were fashionable in the late sixties with a TV set and a record player on the top of one the cupboards and some records stacked beneath. The bookshelves are full, with an occasional gap for family photographs. The room is lit by late September sunshine.

LACI has regularly handsome features with salt and pepper hair, wearing an open-neck shirt without a tie. He is sitting in one of the armchairs, smoking a cigarette and reading a newspaper with a pair of glasses.

VERA. (*Off-stage, through the open kitchen door*) Do you think we're going to recognise him?
LACI. (*Remains silent.*)
VERA. Laci, can't you hear? I'm talking to you.
LACI. I know.
VERA. Why don't you answer? Do you think . . .
LACI. Have you read the paper? Nothing happens for ages and then suddenly! – there's a lot to read! One can hardly keep up with events.

(VERA *enters, wearing an apron over a summer dress. She is heavy, but not fat; without make-up she looks her age, but her dark hair has recently had an outing to the hairdresser*)

VERA. The third time . . . Do you think?
LACI. (*Reluctantly lowering the newspaper*) I don't know. I remember . . .
VERA. What?

LACI. The way he walked. His hair falling over his forehead. When he was nervous he always tried to sweep it back. He was always well-scrubbed and quite smart. As a teenager, I tried to imitate him, but I was not as smart he was. I didn't have the clothes he had. And come to think of it, I remember his eyes.

VERA. His eyes?

LACI. They were blue.

VERA. What colour are mine?

LACI. Yours? (*Looking at Vera to find out*) Brown.

VERA. They are green.

LACI. They changed.

VERA. Only babies' eyes do. (*Pause.*) He must have changed.

LACI. Yes. We all have.

VERA. (*Sits down opposite* LACI) You haven't. Not much.

LACI. Don't be ridiculous. Does it matter?

VERA. It does. Particularly for a woman.

LACI. Perhaps. Remember the graduation reunion?

VERA. Yours or mine?

LACI. Mine. (*Pause.*) An ugly fat woman shuffled up to me, looked at me up and down and asked point blank: 'Do you know who I am?' I hadn't the faintest idea. When she told me I couldn't believe it; she was one of the most attractive girls in the year. I nearly died of embarrassment.

VERA. More beautiful than Marian?

LACI. You aren't jealous?

VERA. Should I be?

LACI. Why do you ask these questions?

VERA. Shouldn't I? I'm concerned about her.

LACI. Why? You always seem to be concerned about one thing or another.

VERA. I have a reason, don't you think? She doesn't look well these days. She's lost some of her sparkle, her sense of fun. I had coffee with her last week; she was really exhausted. Do you think she and Robi will get on?

LACI. How would I know? You're asking these questions to which you know we don't have the answers. Occasionally I feel that our life is an extension of your work.

VERA. Don't be silly. (*Pause.*) Do you have a picture of him?

LACI. Another question. No, I don't have any photograph apart from the one you've seen.

VERA. The one with you and Marian?

LACI. Yes. The one with me and Marian.

VERA. Nothing since then?

LACI. Vera, stop, please. Nothing since then. No photos, no letters, nothing. Only that single snapshot. And the letter a fortnight ago, saying, he was coming and would like to see me.

VERA. Not us?

LACI. He doesn't know I'm married.

VERA. By your age people usually are.

LACI. Not everybody.

VERA. Is he?

LACI. I don't know. But if he is, he's coming without his wife.

VERA. Why?

LACI. He uses first person singular, as in: 'I'll be visiting the old country...' and 'I'd like to see you...' (*Pause.*) Satisfied?

VERA. In case, he turns up with a wife, there'll be more than enough food.

LACI. No doubt. You always over-cater. I could do with a glass of wine now.

VERA. Don't you think we should wait until...

LACI. Yes, perhaps we should.

(*Silence.*)

VERA. Are you nervous?

LACI. Why should I be?

VERA. You're going to meet a close friend who you haven't seen for... Let me see...

LACI. . . . for a long time.

VERA. It's been a long time.

LACI. Yes.

VERA. (*Walks towards the kitchen*) I should be getting on.

LACI. What are you cooking?

VERA. Your favourites.

LACI. You should be cooking his favourites.

VERA. If I knew . . .

LACI. It'll be delicious whatever you do.

VERA. Laci, that's a first.

LACI. First?

VERA. The first nice thing you've said all day.

LACI. It's still quite early.

VERA. Have you put the champagne in the fridge?

LACI. Yes, I have.

(VERA *leaves the room.* LACI *settles back to read the paper.*)

(*Silence.*)

VERA. (*Opens the kitchen door*) Don't you think you should lay the table?

LACI. Can I finish this article, please? We can wait until . . .

(*Doorbell.* VERA, *after having removed her apron, enters the room.*)

VERA. He's arrived.

LACI. Yes.

VERA. (*Seeing that* LACI *does not move*) What are you waiting for? Open the door.

LACI. Of course. (*He leaves the room.*)

(*Silence.*)

LACI. (*Off-stage*) Robi!

ROBI. (*Off-stage*) Laci, I can't believe . . .

LACI. Do come in.

(ROBI *enters. He is taller than* LACI, *and looks younger than his age. He is wearing a pair of jeans and a light linen jacket with a tie: all look expensive and in good taste. In one hand he is holding a bouquet of flowers, in the other a slim paper bag.*)

ROBI. I can't believe . . .

(*The two men looking at each other as if mesmerised. They make a clumsy attempt to embrace each other but* ROBI *is prevented by the presents he carries.*)

LACI. My wife, Vera. Vera, this is Robi.

VERA. An entirely unnecessary introduction. I've heard so much about you.

ROBI. I hope, not too much. Can I just unload? (*Handing the flowers to* VERA). To the lady of the house. I've bought them this morning but in this heat . . .

VERA. Thank you. They're lovely.

ROBI. (*Handing the paper bag to* LACI.) And this is for you.

LACI. (*Looking inside the bag, pulls out a bottle of whisky*) Great. Thank you.

ROBI. You didn't even look.

LACI. I did. It's a malt.

ROBI. Yes. I remembered you liked whisky all those years ago.

VERA. Did you? I didn't know.

LACI. This must be the only thing you don't know about me.

VERA. Why don't we sit down?

(*They all sit down.*)

ROBI. (*Looking at Laci.*) You haven't changed.

VERA. Didn't I tell you?

LACI. Of course, I have. What you mean is you can still recognise me. (*Pause.*) To return the compliment you look like being on the top of the world.

ROBI. I wouldn't know, but at least I've recovered from the jet lag.

VERA. It must have been a great journey. I've never been outside Europe. How long did the journey take?

ROBI. I changed planes in London. Six hours from New York, and then another two to Budapest. I can assure you long-haul air journeys are not fun. I can say this, since I've travelled a great deal both for business and pleasure.

VERA. Anyway, I envy you. Let's open a bottle of champagne to celebrate your homecoming.

LACI. It's not French, only local.

ROBI. It's perfectly all right; I had some of the stuff earlier this week.

LACI. When did you arrive?

ROBI. A week ago.

LACI. And how long are you staying?

ROBI. A few more days.

VERA. Is it not too short after such a long time?

ROBI. I have to get back.

VERA. Laci, will you?

(LACI *disappears in the kitchen.*)

ROBI. (*Looking at the pictures on display*) Are these your children? They're lovely.

VERA. No. They're my sister's. We don't have children.

(LACI *returns with a tray, holding a bottle of champagne and four glasses. He opens the bottle, proceeds to pour it into three glasses and hands one glass each to* VERA *and* ROBI, *who stand up.*)

VERA AND LACI. Welcome home.

ROBI. Thank you. To your health.

(*They all drink.*)

ROBI. Are we expecting someone else?

VERA. Why do you ask?

ROBI. The fourth glass.

VERA. Laci, now you spoilt it.

ROBI. Who is it?

LACI. It's a surprise. Anyway, the other guest may not come.

VERA. Isn't this lovely? I'm not a great champagne drinker but it's very refreshing in this weather.

LACI. Such a heat wave at the end of September is quite unusual.

ROBI. I'm quite accustomed to eccentric weather.

LACI. Why?

ROBI. A May snowstorm, a devastating autumn tornado or unseasonably high temperatures in winter isn't at all unusual in New York.

VERA. Funny talking about weather.

ROBI. The greatest lubricant of human communication.

VERA. You sound like an advertising man.

ROBI. Now that's funny.

LACI. Why?

ROBI. Because I am in advertising.

VERA. But you said in your letter . . .

LACI. . . . that you finished law school.

VERA. Where?

ROBI. In Harvard.

VERA. Harvard? That's one of the best.

ROBI. My alma mater should be ever so proud. Its fame of excellence has spread even into the People's Republic of Hungary.

LACI. Vera would know. She's in the trade.

ROBI. (*to* VERA) Are you a solicitor?

VERA. No. Not a solicitor. (*Pause.*) I happen to be a judge.

ROBI. Ah. A judge? It can't be easy here. (*Pause.*) Considering the political pressures.

VERA. One tries, you know. One has to be fair. It's not always easy to be honest.

LACI. (*Interrupting*) Let's not talk about work now.

(*Silence.*)

ROBI. You have a lovely flat. (*He walks upstage towards the lights and looking at the audience*) What a fantastic view! I didn't realise . . . The Danube, the bridges, the Royal Castle.

LACI. Yes, we're on the fourth floor.

VERA. It's less marvellous when the lift doesn't work. On average twice a week.

LACI. I bet that wouldn't happen in New York.

VERA. Well, what about the great blackout? Whenever it was.

ROBI. In 1965, I think. In the States nothing is on a small scale. The birth rates went up nine months later. (*Pause.*) However, credit should go where credit's due. They've done an amazing job. When I left, the city was in ruins.

LACI. An amazing job? Yes, at a cost. The country has massive debts. Unimaginable. Up to our necks.

VERA. Laci, why should you see the negative side of everything?

LACI. What are you talking about?

VERA. Don't pretend. The future, the country, your job . . .

(*The doorbell rings. They are all relieved.* LACI *and* VERA *jump up.*)

VERA. Laci, you go.

LACI. (*Leaves the room.*)

MARIAN. (*Offstage*) Hello Laci. Am I late?

LACI. (*Offstage*) No, right on time. (*Pause.*) Come in. There's a surprise for you.

MARIAN. (*Offstage*) I don't like surprises.

LACI. (*Offstage*) Shut up. Close your eyes.

(LACI *and* MARIAN *enter the room.* LACI *is leading* MARIAN *by her hand; she has closed her eyes, and* LACI *gesticulates with his index finger over his mouth to the other two to keep quiet.*)

LACI. Now open your eyes.

MARIAN. (*An attractive woman, looks younger than her age, her shoulder length hair is freshly coiffed, wears a simple well-cut linen dress and flat-soled canvas shoes. For a second she stands paralysed, then she opens her arms and walks towards Robi.*) Jesus Christ!

ROBI. No Marian, it's only me. (*He walks to Marian, they embrace and kiss each other.*)

MARIAN. I can't believe it. Is that really you?

VERA. (*Walks to the tray and pours champagne into the fourth glass, and wants to hand it to Marian.*) We should drink to . . .

MARIAN. (*Takes the glass from* VERA.) Just a minute. (*Pause.*) I still can't believe . . . I really can't.

LACI. What?

MARIAN. That Robi has turned up. After all this time.

VERA. Come on, Marian. (*She raises her glass*) We should drink to Robi.

MARIAN. To Robi.

ROBI. Well, believe it or not, here I am.

LACI. Like old times. (*Pause.*) Nothing has changed.

MARIAN. Haven't you seen the roundabout?

LACI. Of course. We pass it at least once a week. Why?

VERA. What?

MARIAN. There isn't a red star any more.

VERA. I'm not surprised.

MARIAN. Overnight someone mowed down the five arms, leaving a red circle.

ROBI. What is this all about?

MARIAN. You know the roundabout at the Buda side of the Chain Bridge? You must remember . . .

ROBI. Remember what?

MARIAN. In the summer, year after year, the large circular
flowerbed in the middle of the roundabout had a star com-
posed of red salvias.

ROBI. What I remember was a bomb site.

LACI. Well done.

VERA. Is it?

LACI. Yes.

MARIAN. (*To* ROBI) Vera disapproves.

VERA. No, I don't. (*Pause.*) I'm just concerned.

MARIAN. Concerned about what?

LACI. (*Crossing the room to the tray and fills the glasses*) Why
don't I fill your glasses?

ROBI. A brilliant idea.

VERA. Not for me. (*Pause.*) Shall we sit down?

(*They all sit down.*)

LACI. End of the bottle.

VERA. There is a bottle of white in the fridge.

(*The telephone rings.*)

LACI. (*Picks up the receiver*) Yes. (*Pause.*) Sorry, I can't hear
you. Who is it? (*Pause.*) Oh, is that you? (*Pause.*) I'll get
her. (*He hands the receiver to* VERA.) It's for you. (LACI
joins the other two, and they drink more champagne.)

VERA. Yes. (*Pause.*) Sorry I can hardly hear you. (*Pause.*)
It's not a very good time. We've got visitors. (*Pause.*) Why
don't you call tomorrow night? Bye. (*She puts down the
receiver.*)

LACI. Didn't I tell you? I don't want him to ring again. Not
when I am here.

VERA. Sorry, I really can't tell him when to ring.

ROBI. What is this about?

MARIAN. There're always people who make nuisance calls.

LACI. How did he get our number? We're ex-directory.

VERA. I don't know.

LACI. Did you give it to him?

VERA. No, I didn't.

MARIAN. Who was it?

LACI. Never mind.

MARIAN. Why don't you tell us?

VERA. Shall we just forget about it?

MARIAN. I have a guess.

LACI. This wasn't, but occasionally we get calls from people who have appeared in Vera's court and feel aggrieved.

ROBI. Is the judiciary independent?

VERA. It's a complex question.

MARIAN. You're asking the wrong person. She'll, of course, say yes. But if you ask those who were condemned innocently over the years, you might get a different answer.

VERA. Marian, dear, could you just stick to your own field of expertise?

LACI. It's not what it used to be when you left. Things have improved, to be fair.

MARIAN. These days we don't have show trials. Or send you to prison if you don't tow the Party line.

VERA. It's all changed.

MARIAN. We all worship in a broad church now. The slogan is: 'Who is not against us, is with us.'

ROBI. Indifference doesn't necessarily mean support.

MARIAN. Exactly.

LACI. The whole edifice is collapsing now.

VERA. I'm not so sure.

LACI. (*Nervously lights a cigarette and offers it to the others*) Anyone?

ROBI. Thank you, I don't smoke.

VERA. (*to* LACI.) You should follow your friend's example.

LACI. You used to.

ROBI. Not any more. Everyone is now more conscious of their health.

VERA. Not surprising, considering the terrible epidemic.

MARIAN. (*Takes one*) Thank you.

LACI. You see the doctor smokes too.

MARIAN. I know I shouldn't.

VERA. I have the occasional one but Laci manages to get through more than one packet a day. It causes lung cancer.

LACI. You have to die of something.

MARIAN. I'd definitely advise against dying of lung cancer. Messy business. Choose something else.

LACI. I already have. (*Pause.*) Shall we open the bottle of white? It's lovely: dry and light with a hint of a fleeting fragrance. (*Pause.*) This vintage is like drinking an early spring dawn.

MARIAN. What a lovely poetic turn of phrase!

VERA. (*to* ROBI) It must be your presence.

ROBI. Are you writing poetry in secret?

LACI. I wanted too when I was young.

ROBI. At school you were brilliant with words. You got a prize for one of your essays.

LACI. Fancy you remembering that. Shall I get the bottle?

VERA. I'll get it. I have to check something in the kitchen.

(VERA *leaves the room.*)

ROBI. You have a great wife.

MARIAN. You might also say Vera has a great husband.

LACI. Marian, be serious for once.

ROBI. How long have you been married?

LACI. Twenty-seven years.

ROBI. Twenty-seven years? (*Pause.*) Such a long time.

MARIAN. You make it sound like a prison sentence. Meted out by Vera.

LACI. Do I?

ROBI. Do you have children?

MARIAN. Where is the wine?

LACI. Marian don't be silly. It's perfectly all right. It was such a long time ago.

ROBI. Sorry, I didn't want to . . .

LACI. We had a son. (*He lights another cigarette.*) He died aged four. Sarcoma of the bone.

MARIAN. Sarcoma is . . .

ROBI. I know what sarcoma is. (*Pause.*) I know very well what sarcoma is.

MARIAN. Sorry.

LACI. It was a difficult birth. Caesarean. (*Pause.*) After that Vera decided not to have more children. (*Pause.*) And I agreed. I . . .

ROBI. Have you regretted it?

VERA. (*Enters, holding a bottle of wine*) Here comes the early spring dawn. Laci, will you open it?

(LACI *opens the bottle, pours the wine into four glasses; they all taste it.*)

MARIAN. Delicious. Where did you buy it?

LACI. I didn't. An Easter present from one of my pupils' father. They have a small vineyard on the northern slopes of Lake Balaton.

MARIAN. I wish my patients would bring me wine like this.

ROBI. Lake Balaton? Do you remember?

LACI. Yes, I do.

VERA. Don't interrupt him. You don't even know what he's going to say.

LACI. Yes, I do.

ROBI. Our excursion during the spring of the last year at school?

MARIAN. Yes, I do too. (*Pause.*) Even talking about it makes me feel old.

ROBI. Climbing up a hillside, we came across a little stream. Being thirsty after lunch, Laci declared we must drink from the crystal-clear water. So healthy for you. And we all did. Remember?

MARIAN. Yes.

ROBI. As we followed the winding path uphill, at the next turning we came upon a couple of young sporty types who were pissing into the same stream.

LACI. It was fun.

ROBI. Yes. It was.

(*Silence.*)

VERA. When do you want to eat? I have to prepare something a few minutes before.

ROBI. What are we going to eat?

VERA. I didn't know your favourite dish, and your friends were not much help either.

LACI. I'm sure you'll like it.

VERA. I wouldn't bet on it.

MARIAN. Don't listen to her. She's a marvellous cook.

VERA. You are having clear chicken soup with angel hair pasta, tiny pieces of chicken breast and julienne of vegetables and a veal casserole.

ROBI. You sound like a professional cook. Veal?

VERA. Don't you like it?

ROBI. It's my favourite.

VERA. It's Laci's, too.

MARIAN. They always had similar taste.

VERA. They both were in love with you.

LACI. We were friends.

ROBI. Yes.

MARIAN. All very proper. Platonic.

ROBI. Yes.

VERA. (*to* MARIAN.) You sound disappointed.

MARIAN. Do I?

LACI. The three of us . . . We were together a lot.

ROBI. Yes, we were.

(*Silence.*)

MARIAN. Vera, I've given your number to the hospital switch-board. Do you mind?

VERA. Of course not.

LACI. Are you on duty?

MARIAN. No, but I have a young patient with cardiac insufficiency who managed to pick up an infection, probably from one of his visitors.

VERA. As if there weren't enough microbes in the hospital.

MARIAN. Not very complimentary about my great profession.

VERA. More than you are about mine.

LACI. Don't you argue again.

ROBI. It's only professional pride.

LACI. Whatever it is, avoid both hospitals and courts at all cost.

MARIAN. Silly advice.

LACI. Why?

VERA. If people followed it, we would both starve.

ROBI. (*to* MARIAN) So you were admitted to medical school after all?

MARIAN. It would have been difficult to get a consultant job otherwise.

ROBI. You're a consultant now?

MARIAN. Yes. For several years.

ROBI. Of course. How stupid of me.

MARIAN. Nothing 'of-course' about it. (*Pause.*) I can assure you, it wasn't easy.

ROBI. Why?

MARIAN. Why don't you ask Vera?

LACI. Leave her out of this, will you Marian?

VERA. Marian's family was classified as 'class alien'.

MARIAN. And consequently I became the enemy of the people.

VERA. Not quite. But it didn't make for an easy career.

ROBI. But that's ridiculous.

LACI. It is.

ROBI. I've thought that this nonsense stopped a long time ago.

VERA. It had.

MARIAN. At the beginning of '57 it was all different. Lucky you – you wouldn't know. You'd gone.

ROBI. Is this a reproach?

MARIAN. Only an observation.

ROBI. You seem to have forgotten something.

MARIAN. Have I?

ROBI. Yes.

MARIAN. What?

(*Silence.*)

ROBI. I asked you to come with me.

LACI. Did he?

MARIAN. Yes, he did.

VERA. Marian?

MARIAN. I didn't, obviously.

VERA. Did you regret it?

MARIAN. I don't know. It doesn't matter now, does it?

LACI. You never told me.

MARIAN. No.

LACI. Why?

MARIAN. Do you tell me everything?

ROBI. Why didn't you come with me? I begged you.

MARIAN. I don't know. (*Pause.*) And if I did?

ROBI. I might have had a different life.

MARIAN. Shall we just forget it? Otherwise we'll be visitors in our pasts. Laci, can I have a little more wine?

LACI. (*Stands up, pours wine into* MARIAN's *glass*) Robi, a top-up?

ROBI. No, thank you. I'm fine.

VERA. (*Seeing* LACI *approaching her*) No, I have to get lunch.

MARIAN. (*to* ROBI) Do you really want to know?

ROBI. Yes.

MARIAN. I didn't want to leave my family. (*Pause.*) And I hoped I could study medicine in the end.

ROBI. Is this your excuse?

MARIAN. I don't need an excuse. It's an explanation.

ROBI. You would have got into any medical school in the world.

MARIAN. Perhaps. But there was something else.

(*Silence.*)

(ROBI *stands up, walks to* MARIAN *and puts his hand on her shoulder.*)

ROBI. Marian?

MARIAN. My father was interned.

ROBI. Was he sent to a camp?

MARIAN. Yes. Sounds strange, doesn't it? Interned.

ROBI. But I thought that had stopped.

LACI. Not until after the restoration of Communism.

ROBI. But why on earth was he interned?

MARIAN. A very good question.

ROBI. Your father was a surgeon, wasn't he?

MARIAN. Yes. (*Pause.*) He was interned for what Vera would call 'counter-revolutionary' activity.

ROBI. Revolution.

LACI. Yes.

VERA. Let's not argue . . .

ROBI. Your father wasn't a revolutionary?

MARIAN. He wasn't.

ROBI. I remember he warned us about going to that demonstration . . .

LACI. . . . which had started it all.

VERA. And despite that, you all went?

LACI. Yes.

ROBI. And you, Vera? What did you do on that day?

VERA. I decided to stay at home. (*Pause.*) I knew it was going to end in tears.

MARIAN. Well, it did.

LACI. Tears? In blood rather than in tears.

VERA. Do you want to know the truth? (*Pause.*) I didn't approve. And do you want to know why? Because without the Communists, I wouldn't have become a lawyer. Not with my background.

MARIAN. Don't exaggerate.

VERA. Do I? Do you think the peasant girl from a village in the middle of nowhere would have been admitted to university? Not in a hundred years.

MARIAN. You're listening to the only true Communist in the country.

LACI. Don't be silly.

ROBI. In '56 we thought we were changing the world.

MARIAN. In a way, we were.

LACI. For twelve days.

ROBI. (*to* MARIAN) Your father? What happened to him?

MARIAN. My father went to help medical emergencies. (*Pause.*) On the wrong side of the barricade.

ROBI. And for this he was interned?

MARIAN. Well, not quite. (*Pause.*) After the fighting ended, they came for him.

ROBI. They?

MARIAN. Robi, you are getting irritating. Have you forgotten? Do you think they had a card to introduce themselves?

ROBI. Sorry.

MARIAN. Or a warrant for that matter?

VERA. It was an emergency.

MARIAN. He was forced to confess to crimes he didn't commit.

ROBI. What was the charge?

VERA. It wasn't a formal charge.

MARIAN. He was accused of helping the counter-revolutionaries.

ROBI. But he was only . . .

MARIAN. . . . helping the wounded by improvising in the middle of street fighting.

ROBI. But surely that isn't a crime.

MARIAN. Well, it was then. (*Pause.*) He refused to confess. (*Pause.*) He was beaten up. While in the prison, he suffered a stroke. He was saved by one of his colleagues, a neurologist who fought to get him into his clinic. When he was discharged, my parents were interned. For three years. By then, restoration completed . . .

VERA. (*Interrupting*) It wasn't restoration of the Stalinist system.

LACI. Let's not get into this again.

MARIAN. . . . they could move back to Budapest.

ROBI. What a dreadful story. Poor you.

MARIAN. It's not quite the end. A little post-script which says volumes of our shining system. Last week, I decided to get my dad's medical notes from the neurological clinic. I know the current director quite well and asked for them. He came back a couple of days later. And surprise, surprise. The only file missing in that year was my dad's.

VERA. It could have been lost.

MARIAN. Really?

LACI. It could have been, but probably wasn't.

MARIAN. Bloody right. It was removed, and probably destroyed.

VERA. You don't know that.

ROBI. Why was it removed?

MARIAN. To destroy evidence.

VERA. Your father wasn't an important person. He was a professional man caught up . . .

MARIAN. Never mind Vera. (*Pause.*) If we have free elections . . .

LACI. That's a big if.

MARIAN. We shall Laci; have no doubts.

ROBI. It was amazing to watch on TV the East Germans driving their Trabis or simply walking through the border with Austria. It's the beginning of the end.

VERA. Don't bank on it.

LACI. I'm afraid Vera might be right.

MARIAN. Her wishful thinking . . .

VERA. Marian, don't be nasty.

MARIAN. I would bet the Berlin Wall will come down before the end of the year.

ROBI. Let's drink to the collapse of the Berlin Wall.

LACI. Hang on. I have to fill your glasses.

VERA. Let me do it this time. (*She gets the bottle and fills their glasses.*)

LACI. And you?

VERA. I still have enough.

MARIAN, LACI, ROBI. (*Stand up, lifting their glasses*) To the fall of the Berlin Wall.

LACI. Come on, Vera, don't be a spoilsport.

VERA. (*Joins them reluctantly*) Cheers. (*Pause.*) And after?

MARIAN. What do you mean? After? (*Pause.*) Europe will be free.

ROBI. A continent at peace with itself. (*Pause.*) Perhaps a new golden age.

VERA. Do you think so?

ROBI. I do.

(*Silence.*)

MARIAN. I want to ask Robi . . .

LACI. I know what you want to ask.

MARIAN. Do you?

LACI. Yes.

MARIAN. I doubt it.

LACI. Do you want a bet?

MARIAN. Dinner in your favourite restaurant.

LACI. It's a deal.

(*Silence.*)

MARIAN. Come on.

LACI. (*turning to* ROBI) We know why you left . . .

VERA. You may, but I don't.

MARIAN. You might have guessed . . .

LACI. . . . but we don't know why you haven't come home for over thirty years.

MARIAN. You won.

(*Silence.*)

VERA. Come on Robi, we want to know.

ROBI. First, I should correct the question.

LACI. What's wrong with it?

ROBI. I didn't come home. This is not my home.

(*Silence.*)

VERA. How can you say this? You were born here, went to school here . . .

LACI. And this is your mother tongue.

ROBI. Yes. (*Pause.*) What you've just said is all true. (*Pause.*) But . . .

MARIAN. Come on Robi, spit it out.

ROBI. I've been living in America for decades. I was educated there. I have my professional life there. (*Pause.*) My home is America. Or to be precise New York. I love that city. I'm not sure I would want to live in Kansas City, Fort Worth or anywhere else for that matter.

LACI. You still haven't . . .

ROBI. (*interrupting*) Sorry, Laci. I haven't come back for the simple reason I didn't want to.

LACI. But why?

ROBI. (looking at LACI) Funny, you're asking this.

LACI. I don't understand . . .

ROBI. Don't you? (*Pause.*) When we left, I made a resolution.

MARIAN. Which was?

ROBI. I wouldn't come back while the same system of oppression existed. While still they call '56 a 'counter-revolution'.

MARIAN. It was a bit of a gamble.

ROBI. Yes, it was.

LACI. It has paid off now.

VERA. It mightn't have . . .

MARIAN. . . . and then we wouldn't have seen you again.

ROBI. You could have visited me.

LACI. Didn't it occur to you to change your mind?

ROBI. It did. (*Pause.*) Once.

MARIAN. When?

ROBI. When my parents came back for the first time.

VERA. Do you hate this country so much?

ROBI. I don't hate the country, but I hate what people had done to it. (*Pause.*) I wanted to have a complete break. (*Pause.*) With everything and everybody.

(*Silence.*)

LACI. And this included us, me and Marian?

(*Silence.*)

ROBI. Yes.

LACI. Why?

MARIAN. Laci, you shouldn't ask. (*Pause.*) We may know one day.

ROBI. Yes.

(*Silence.*)

VERA. When did your parents visit the first time?

ROBI. I think it was towards the end of the seventies.

LACI. So late?

ROBI. Yes. (*Pause.*) My father was sentenced – in absentia – fortunately.

VERA. To twelve years.

(*They all look at her in silence.*)

ROBI. (*agitated*) How do you know?

MARIAN. Now, Robi, that's a stupid question. Have you forgotten? You obviously have. They've kept files on us.

ROBI. I don't know.

MARIAN. Don't you?

VERA. Marian, calm down.

MARIAN. Why should I? (*Pause.*) According to Vera, it's perfectly acceptable that there has been and there is a state-sponsored system of informers, and a file is kept on us of what we do, what we say.

VERA. I don't dispute that.

ROBI. Vera, I really want to know.

VERA. If Marian didn't interrupt me . . . (*Pause.*) I can assure you there is nothing sinister about it. (*Pause.*) When I was appointed judge, I had access to the files of some of the post-'56 trials.

ROBI. Had you?

VERA. The purpose of this exercise was to identify those cases that would be considered for rehabilitation at a later stage. (*Pause.*) And this is how I came across your father's file.

ROBI. I should apologise.

VERA. There is no need.

ROBI. He was elected to be a member of the National Council of our district in the heady days of late October.

VERA. I know.

MARIAN. Didn't you think it was ridiculous?

VERA. Not at the time.

MARIAN. You always find an excuse.

ROBI. This was the reason why he decided we should leave.

VERA. The only reason?

LACI. You shouldn't cross examine.

ROBI. He disliked the system.

VERA. Let it lie there.

MARIAN. You're being rather cryptic, Vera. Unlike your usual straightforward, bang in the middle, going for the jugular, self.

LACI. So you came back because the system is collapsing.

ROBI. Yes.

LACI. Why didn't you write?

MARIAN. To any of us?

ROBI. I don't know.

MARIAN. There must be an explanation.

VERA. Who is being inquisitive now?

MARIAN. Considering that we've grown up together . . .

LACI. . . . we're entitled to know why our best friend didn't bother.

MARIAN. We're entitled to nothing. (*Pause.*) But it would be nice to know. (*Pause.*) Robi dear . . .

ROBI. One night I went home and told my father I was leaving.

MARIAN. Just like that. Out of the blue.

ROBI. Not quite.

MARIAN. Something happened.

ROBI. Yes.

VERA. Many people decided to go.

LACI. Had everybody emigrated who had been fed up, the country would have been deserted.

ROBI. I had a very good reason to leave.

LACI. I'm sorry, I didn't want to . . .

ROBI. My father was not a counter-revolutionary, and he didn't blow up Russian tanks.

VERA. Remind me of his job?

ROBI. He was a solicitor.

VERA. Of course. (*Pause.*) He had access to confidential information of clients.

ROBI. Yes, I guess so.

(*The doorbell rings.*)

LACI. I hope it's not him.

VERA. Relax. I've told him not to come here ever again. (*Pause.*) We don't expect anybody. It must be one of the neighbours.

LACI. I'll go.

VERA. (*Leaves the room, leaving the door to the hall ajar*) Stay with your friends.

MARIAN. Laci, are you all right?

VERA. (*Offstage*) Hi. Would you like to come in?

(*We can't hear the caller's reply.*)

VERA. Oh, not again. I'll tell him. Thank you. Goodbye. (*She enters the room, from the door*) Laci, you left the car window open. Again.

LACI. I'm sorry. I'll go down straightaway. Where's the key?

VERA. Where it always is.

LACI. When it isn't somewhere else.

VERA. Very funny. Could you just go?

LACI. (*Leaving the room*) Yes.

MARIAN. (*to* VERA) Is he all right?

ROBI. Shouldn't he be?

VERA. Robi should know.

MARIAN. Yes, he should.

VERA. Laci is unwell from time to time.

ROBI. What do you mean?

VERA. He suffers from depression.

ROBI. So sorry. Is it serious?

VERA. Yes. It's not just feeling blue from time to time. It's not the occasional frustration of not being able to cope. It's not the hour of the wolves' depression of waking up in the middle of night, a depression which lifts with the dawn and evaporates with your morning shower. (*Pause.*) It's not even the depression middle-aged people may have.

ROBI. Vera, you told us what it isn't. Will you just spit it out.

VERA. Laci has severe clinical depression. He is on medication.

ROBI. For how long?

VERA. It must have started well before we met.

MARIAN. For more than 30 years. We can't blame Vera for it.

VERA. It's no time to be funny.

MARIAN. When you want to scream your head off in anger or frustration, perhaps it's time to laugh. (*Pause.*) There is something else. (*Looking at* VERA.) Shall I?

VERA. Yes. Robi should know.

(*They hear the key turning in the lock and opening the door of the flat.*)

LACI. (*Enters*) It's all done.

VERA. Anything missing?

LACI. Nothing. Nothing at all.

VERA. We're lucky. Last time they stole everything from the car. Including a half-eaten chocolate bar.

LACI. Anyone for more wine? (*Looking at the bottle*) There's a little left.

MARIAN. (*Holding her glass towards* LACI, *who refills it*) I wouldn't mind. Just half . . . Thank you.

ROBI. No, thanks. (*Pause.*) It's great to see you Laci. (*Pause.*) And you Marian. (*Pause.*) And meeting Vera.

VERA. How did you get to the States?

ROBI. We took the train to the border, each of us carrying a small suitcase with the essentials. My mum sewed some jewellery under the lining of her coat, and my father had some dollars hidden away.

VERA. Where did your father get the dollars?

ROBI. I don't know. He didn't tell me.

LACI. Vera, don't interrupt.

ROBI. From the station we just walked through the border to Austria. Like the East Germans are doing now.

MARIAN. It couldn't have been so easy.

ROBI. Well, not quite. Although there was no border control, we had to avoid mines and barbed wire. We hired a guide.

MARIAN. A little excursion.

ROBI. We stayed outside Vienna in a refugee camp for two months, were put on a waiting list and when our number came up we were allowed to go to the US. (*Pause.*) The rest you know.

MARIAN. Not really, but never mind.

ROBI. I learned English at an intensive course.

LACI. But you already spoke . . .

MARIAN. It's rather different to speak English in Budapest and in New York.

ROBI. Then I graduated from law school.

VERA. Previously you said you were in advertising.

ROBI. Well, yes and no.

VERA. What do you actually do?

ROBI. I work for a law firm. We specialise in drawing up contracts for artists, amongst other things. I liaise with a large PR firm in Madison Avenue to raise money for the Metropolitan Museum of Art. I supervise endowments.

LACI. Endowments?

ROBI. Donations. Legacies. Awards. Giving money.

LACI. Sort of charity?

ROBI. Yes.

LACI. How much money is involved?

ROBI. A great deal. As much as we can get.

LACI. Hundreds of dollars? Thousands?

ROBI. Are you joking? Add a few zeros. We like to think in terms of hundreds of thousands or much better, millions.

LACI. No one has so much money.

ROBI. You'd be surprised. New York is a rich city. If you give a couple of hundred thousand, they may name a room after you. If you give a hundred million, well, your name might be etched on the façade of a new wing.

VERA. We're lucky in this country, we don't need . . .

ROBI. You think so?

VERA. Yes.

ROBI. I wouldn't be so sure.

VERA. Why?

ROBI. Here the state subsidises art, which is fine. But there is a price to pay.

VERA. And that is?

ROBI. They tell you what to do. They are paying for it.

VERA. Not now.

ROBI. Are you sure?

MARIAN. It has got better.

ROBI. Better?

MARIAN. Yes. Gradually.

LACI. Do you like your job?

ROBI. I do. Very much. It's fun. I meet all sorts of people.

VERA. Do you?

ROBI. What do you mean?

VERA. If you are after millionaires' money . . .

ROBI. You'd be surprised. I've met some extraordinary characters. (*Pause.*) I've also started to work for a charity.

MARIAN. What sort of charity?

ROBI. AIDS.

VERA. AIDS? We have cases here, but not on the scale you have in the States.

ROBI. I know the statistics . . .

LACI. So you have two jobs?

ROBI. Not really. The AIDS charity is voluntary work.

VERA. (*Looking at her watch*) It's after one; I think we should eat. Aren't you hungry?

LACI. I'm starving.

VERA. (*Leaving for the kitchen*) It won't be long.

MARIAN. Robi, are you married?

LACI. Why do you ask?

MARIAN. For two reasons. You came alone. And I'm interested.

ROBI. No, I'm not.

MARIAN. Are you divorced?

LACI. You're worse than Vera.

MARIAN. Why? Is it wrong to ask that of someone who was once your best friend?

LACI. Sorry, Marian.

MARIAN. Don't apologise. (*Pause.*) Living with a judge makes you feel you're always in the dock.

LACI. No, I'm not.

MARIAN. You'd be both better off if you told her occasionally where to get off.

ROBI. Marian, you're . . .

LACI. Marian and Vera are very good friends.

ROBI. Obviously.

MARIAN. So then Robi, are you divorced?

LACI. Marian, are you drunk?

MARIAN. Of course not. My liver enzymes work like a dream. I could drink a whole bottle before . . .

LACI. Would you like to finish the white? There is a drop or two.

(LACI *stands up and pours the remaining wine into* MARIAN's *glass.*)

MARIAN. Thank you. (*Pause.*) Robi, dear?

ROBI. No, I'm not divorced. (*Pause.*) And to prevent your next question . . .

MARIAN. Are you getting shirty?

ROBI. . . . I live alone.

(*Silence.*)

MARIAN. Are you celibate?

ROBI. Yes.

LACI. Marian, that's really just too much.

MARIAN. Laci, why don't you help Vera while we talk about sex?

LACI. Vera can manage in the kitchen without me.

MARIAN. Such a waste.

LACI. Why do you say that?

MARIAN. Such a handsome man. (*Pause.*) With pots of money.

ROBI. I don't have pots of money.

MARIAN. We all know how much American lawyers earn.

ROBI. Do you? (*Pause.*) I live well, but I'm not rich. Not by American standard, anyway.

LACI. Does it matter?

MARIAN. No, not if you have it.

(*Silence.*)

ROBI. Marian, are you married?

MARIAN. No, I'm not.

ROBI. Why?

MARIAN. Because neither of you married me.

LACI. That's not fair.

MARIAN. Why?

LACI. Because you fancied Robi and not me.

MARIAN. How do you know?

LACI. Never mind. Is it true?

(*Silence.*)

MARIAN. Yes.

LACI. Were you in love with Robi?

ROBI. Laci, this is getting embarrassing.

LACI. I'm sorry.

MARIAN. I was. (*Pause.*) And he knew it.

LACI. How?

MARIAN. I told him.

(*Silence.*)

ROBI. Yes.

LACI. (*Disappearing to the bedroom*) Just a second.

ROBI. Was this necessary?

MARIAN. Are you embarrassed?

ROBI. Should I be?

MARIAN. Truth can be a trap.

LACI. (*Returns, holding a photograph in his hand*) Here it is. Vera dug it up earlier today. (*He hands it to Marian.*)

MARIAN. (*Scrutinising the photo, then handing it to* ROBI) Oh, God.

ROBI. (*Looking at the picture*) When was it taken?

LACI. In the summer, just after the baccalaureate.

MARIAN. Who took the picture?

LACI. My father. He was so happy with his new East German camera. Don't you remember?

ROBI. What happened to him?

LACI. He died. A couple of years after my mother.

(*Silence.*)

ROBI. And your brother?

LACI. He's alive.

ROBI. What does he do?

LACI. He used to work in the Ministry of Internal Affairs.

ROBI. I see.

LACI. We don't see each other.

MARIAN. Why are you lying to Robi?

LACI. I'm not lying.

MARIAN. You're certainly not telling the truth.

LACI. It's a long story. And not one I wanted to talk about today. He was sacked from his job, his marriage fell apart, his two grown-up sons do not want anything to do with him. He's practically destitute.

MARIAN. Was it him who phoned earlier?

LACI. Yes. Vera gives him money from time to time. She thinks we should help him. I don't. I don't want to see him.

MARIAN. Robi, do you know him?

ROBI. Yes. Sort of . . .

MARIAN. You sound mysterious. Never mind. Laci, can I have another look?

LACI. (*handing the picture back to* MARIAN.) Of course.

MARIAN. (*Looking for a minute*) Interesting.

LACI. What?

MARIAN. Look again, you two. (*Pause.*) Do you notice something?

LACI. (*Holding the picture, scrutinising it*) We're all so young.

ROBI. (*Getting the picture from* LACI, *and looking at it*) That's not very surprising. We were eighteen. (*Pause.*) Marian looks ravishing.

MARIAN. That's obvious. (*Pause.*) Something else.

ROBI. Come on, Marian. What is it?

MARIAN. Neither of you noticed it. (*Pause.*) Laci is looking dutifully into the lens. I'm looking at Robi. (*Pause.*) And Robi is looking at you.

(VERA *opens the kitchen door, but off-stage.*)

VERA. Laci, dear, could you lay the table?

LACI. Just a second, I'm coming.

MARIAN. Do you remember the party after the baccalaureate?

ROBI. Yes, I do.

LACI. Me, too.

MARIAN. It was at the party . . .

ROBI. Yes.

MARIAN. . . . . I nearly raped you.

LACI. And this is the reason why Robi escaped from the country.

MARIAN. I didn't know you had a sense of humour.

LACI. Occasionally. When I try.

VERA. (*Shouting from the kitchen*) Laci, are you coming?

MARIAN. (*Shouting*) He's coming. He said something witty and hasn't quite recovered from it.

(LACI *leaves the room.* VERA *and* ROBI *embrace each other, and then separate.*)

MARIAN. It was a long, never-ending summer . . .

ROBI. And so it seemed.

MARIAN. . . . before it all started

ACT TWO

The same room, a couple of hours later, after lunch. MARIAN *and* ROBI *are sitting on the sofa,* MARIAN *smoking.*

LACI. (*standing by the kitchen door*) Vera, do come in. The washing up can wait.

VERA. (*Off*) I'm just putting the leftovers in the fridge. I'll be with you in a second.

LACI. Anyone for a brandy?

ROBI. Don't you think we'd enough to drink?

MARIAN. Come on Robi, don't be spoilsport.

LACI. It's a special occasion. (*Pause.*) When are we going to meet next?

MARIAN. I hope not in another thirty-odd years. We'll be dead long before then.

LACI. Do you think of death?

MARIAN. Yes. (*Pause.*) Being a doctor . . .

LACI. And you, Robi?

ROBI. Shall we talk about something else?

MARIAN. Are you frightened?

ROBI. Yes. (*Pause.*) Of dying. Aren't you?

VERA. (*Having entered earlier*) What a morbid conversation. Let's have a brandy.

LACI. Will you get the glasses?

VERA. (*Disappearing in the kitchen, returns carrying a small try with four glasses*) Here we are.

LACI. (*Having got the brandy bottle, pours it into the glasses*) It's local, but quite drinkable.

ROBI. Just a taste for me.

MARIAN. Robi, you've changed.

ROBI. Yes.

MARIAN. As a student . . .

ROBI. (*Interrupting*) That was different.

MARIAN. Remember, when your mother found a couple of
   vodka bottles in one of your drawers?
ROBI. She was terrified I was becoming an alcoholic. Laci
   definitely helped.
VERA. (*To* LACI) Did you drink a lot?
LACI. Not really. (*Pause.*) Why do you always try to find
   something in my past?
VERA. I just asked.
ROBI. Vera, what a marvellous lunch. Thank you.
VERA. It was nothing special.
MARIAN. It was delicious. Vera, false modesty doesn't suit
   you. You're a great cook. I envy you. (*She raises her glass*)
   Cheers.

(*They all drink.*)

ROBI. (*Raising his glass*) To Vera.
MARIAN AND LACI. To Vera.
MARIAN. You probably could earn a living as a professional
   chef.
VERA. I may have to.
LACI. Vera's concerned she might lose her job.
MARIAN. You won't.
VERA. How do you know?
MARIAN. I don't.

(*Silence.*)

ROBI. Why would you?
VERA. There'll be a change of guard. At all levels. (*Pause.*)
   I'm associated with the old regime. And worse than that.
   I'm *not* apologising about my professional career.
MARIAN. The system may change, but the Hungarians won't.
   I bet, you won't be sacked. But if you are, shall we open a
   restaurant? You cook, I'll be the health inspector and (*nod-
   ding towards* ROBI) Uncle Sam will provide the capital.
LACI. And me?

MARIAN. You'll be the manager.

VERA. Laci? You must be joking.

MARIAN. Wine waiter then.

LACI. That's a deal.

(*Silence.*)

ROBI. (*To Marian*) So you didn't marry?

MARIAN. I thought we closed this subject.

ROBI. I don't want to pry.

MARIAN. You don't. (*Pause.*) But it's boring for Laci and Vera.

LACI. Not really.

MARIAN. Soon after I qualified, I met a neurologist. It was a good match, as they say.

VERA. He was, and still is, a rather handsome man.

MARIAN. Vera fancied him.

VERA. Don't be stupid.

MARIAN. Acknowledging a smidgen of human weakness, doesn't make you any less . . .

VERA. Laci, shall we clean the kitchen?

(VERA *and* LACI *leave the room.*)

MARIAN. For a while we lived in sin, as his very Catholic mother kept reminding us. She was not overenthusiastic that her only son married out.

ROBI. Married out?

MARIAN. Did you forget?

ROBI. Your Jewish background? It was never an issue.

MARIAN. Maybe not for you. But for quite a few people it was. And it still could be now. And don't say Jewish background. It sounds like the milder variety of a disease. I'm Jewish. Full stop. (*Pause.*) Anyway, after we both had been appointed consultants, we bought a flat and got married. And from that time things started to go wrong.

ROBI. Why?

MARIAN. Why do marriages go wrong? Please discuss.

ROBI. Sorry.

MARIAN. Our jobs destroyed our marriage. We hardly saw each other. When he was on duty, I was at home and vice versa.

ROBI. Children?

MARIAN. None.

ROBI. It might have helped.

MARIAN. How do you know? Have you ever thought of having children?

ROBI. I'm not married.

MARIAN. That doesn't preclude the possibility.

ROBI. I don't like children. They unfailingly turn into horrid adults.

MARIAN. A somewhat cynical view.

ROBI. And?

MARIAN. And, and, and. 'And' seems to be your favourite word.

ROBI. Perhaps. It's a word which opens up endless possibilities without any commitment.

MARIAN. *And* we divorced long time ago. He now lives abroad. Like you.

ROBI. In the States?

MARIAN. No, in England. He is a consultant neurologist in a prestigious London hospital. However, we remained friends. I have visited him a couple of times, and he has been home.

ROBI. Do you live alone?

MARIAN. Yes, now. I had an affair with a married man, but I got rid of him last year.

ROBI. Why?

MARIAN. I got fed up. He used me. (*Pause.*) There was something else.

(*Silence.*)

ROBI. Marian, I don't want to . . .

MARIAN. I wanted to have a child. I was getting on. It was my last chance. Finally I got pregnant. (*Pause.*) He forced me to have an abortion.

ROBI. Forced?

MARIAN. It was a sort of moral blackmail. It would ruin his marriage, the lives of his two children, and so on, and so forth.

ROBI. (*Stands up and embraces Marian*) So sorry.

MARIAN. It's all right. I don't need men these days. They are quite dispensable. Believe it or not, I get tremendous satisfaction from my job.

ROBI. I believe you. (*Pause.*) May I ask a question?

MARIAN. It depends.

ROBI. Laci . . .

MARIAN. Laci? I thought you wanted to know more about my sex life.

ROBI. Is Laci all right?

MARIAN. You asked the same question before lunch.

ROBI. Yes. (*Pause.*) I've this feeling.

MARIAN. What?

ROBI. I don't know. (*Pause.*) Unease.

MARIAN. If you ask him, he'll talk about his work. His marriage is not very happy.

ROBI. Why?

MARIAN. Can't you see? (*Pause.*) They're together because there is nothing better.

ROBI. Aren't all marriages like that?

MARIAN. The bachelor's expert view on marriage.

ROBI. After a long time, that is.

MARIAN. Vera doesn't think Laci is good enough for her.

ROBI. Why?

MARIAN. She's very ambitious. (*Pause.*) She doesn't easily make do with second best.

ROBI. Aren't you too harsh?

MARIAN. You asked.

ROBI. Yes. But ...

MARIAN. You don't like the answer, do you? Vera always wanted to get to the top by hook or by crook. And she got there. (*Pause.*) The peasant girl who became a judge. A Communist success story. And now her world is collapsing around her. Her idols are being smashed to smithereens.

ROBI. And Laci?

MARIAN. He's different.

(LACI *and* VERA *return.*)

LACI. All spick and span.

VERA. Not quite, but for a Sunday evening it will do.

MARIAN. Shall we go down for a little walk? It's such a lovely afternoon.

VERA. We haven't had coffee yet. (*Pause.*) And there's something else. (*She leaves and returns from the kitchen with a plate of cakes*) Here it is.

ROBI. (*Looking and the plate*) Strudels!

VERA. Apple, poppy seed and walnut.

ROBI. How did you know?

VERA. Intuition. (*Pause.*) Laci, will you bring plates and forks? I'll get the coffee.

(VERA *and* LACI *leave and return, carrying a tray with a coffee jug, four small cups and saucers, and four plates and forks, respectively.* LACI *hands the plates and forks, while* VERA *pours the coffee.*)

VERA. Anyone for sugar?

MARIAN AND ROBI. No thank you.

(*They all settle around the low table, drinking coffee.*)

ROBI. The real thing. In the States you can drink pints of a hot brown liquid which, by our standards, is hardly recognisable as coffee.

MARIAN. We heard about that.

ROBI. You haven't been to the States?

MARIAN. Of course not.

ROBI. You should come.

MARIAN. Is that an invitation?

ROBI. Yes.

MARIAN. I will.

ROBI. You all should come.

VERA. Thank you. It won't happen in a hurry. (*Pause.*) Please, help yourselves.

(*They all take a piece.*)

ROBI. Poppyseed strudel! In the States it's easier to buy heroin than poppyseed.

MARIAN. Laci, how are you getting on with the book review you're writing for 'And'?

ROBI. 'And'?

LACI. Did you forget the weekly *Life and Literature*?

MARIAN. Robi had already left when the first issue was published.

LACI. Since people said it contained neither life nor literature, everybody called it 'And'.

ROBI. What's the review you are writing?

LACI. George Orwell's *1984*. Have you read it?

ROBI. Yes, it was published ages ago.

MARIAN. Here it was been translated only this year.

ROBI. Not surprising.

MARIAN. In a way, Orwell was wrong.

LACI. Wrong?

MARIAN. Communism has hardly survived beyond 1984.

LACI. It was long enough, don't you think? I feel they stole forty years of our life.

VERA. How can you say that?

(*Silence.*)

ROBI. So, you have a literary career.

LACI. I wouldn't go as far . . .

VERA. Don't be too modest. But you could have done better, if . . .

ROBI. If?

VERA. If he had been a little bit more accommodating.

ROBI. Accommodating?

LACI. I did write a novel when I was twenty-five.

ROBI. About?

LACI. A family saga of three generations starting at the turn of century.

VERA. It was a good story.

LACI. I took it from publisher to publisher. No one would touch it. (*Pause.*) First I didn't know why. Then I realised. One of the more decent publishers suggested certain changes to make it politically more acceptable. I refused.

ROBI. But why?

LACI. My conscience is not for sale.

ROBI. What happened to it?

LACI. I burnt the manuscript. I was bitterly disappointed. I poured my life into it. Like those hospital drips: in the end I was empty. (*Pause.*) Now, I teach literature in a high school and in my spare time . . .

MARIAN. Vera is right; you're too modest.

VERA. You've published a collection of essays and criticism.

LACI. Yes. (*Pause.*) And do you know how many copies were sold?

MARIAN. It wasn't a bestseller, but these books never are. (*Pause.*) It wasn't meant to be.

LACI. Two hundred and twenty-seven. At the last count.

VERA. Why don't you tell Robi?

LACI. Stop prompting me.

VERA. I want to bring the best out of you.

LACI. Since it's so difficult to find it.

VERA. You're very touchy today.

LACI. Sorry.

(*The telephone rings.*)

(VERA *stands up and crosses the room to the 'phone and lifts the receiver.*)

VERA. Hello. (*Pause.*) Yes. (*Pause.*) Yes, she's here. Marian, it's for you.

MARIAN. (*Stands up and walks to the 'phone*) Yes, it's me. (*Silence.*) When? (*Pause.*) I'll come in on the way home. (*Pause.*) Yes. (*Pause.*) Thank you. (*Pause.*) No, don't stay. You've done more than . . . See you tomorrow morning.

VERA. What happened?

MARIAN. The patient I was talking earlier on . . .

VERA. . . . died?

MARIAN. Yes.

ROBI. I'm sorry.

LACI. Yes.

MARIAN. (*Distraught, collapsing in an armchair*) I thought he'd recover. (*Pause.*) A young man . . .

VERA. What happened?

MARIAN. It was probably pulmonary embolus.

LACI. Poor man.

MARIAN. Yes. (*Pause.*) And his poor wife and children.

ROBI. You did everything . . .

MARIAN. (*Interrupting*) How do you know?

ROBI. Sorry.

VERA. You shouldn't take it so personally.

MARIAN. I don't.

VERA. You do. (*Pause.*) How long have you been a doctor? Twenty-five years.

MARIAN. Twenty-seven.

VERA. You must be accustomed to the idea that patients actually die.

LACI. Please, don't argue.

VERA. Whenever a patient of Marian's . . .

LACI. (*Interrupting, raising his voice for the first time*) Can I just for once?

VERA. Sorry.

LACI. Whenever a patient of Marian's dies, Marian dies with them.

(*Silence.*)

MARIAN. That's *not true.*

VERA. You should have a life outside the hospital. (*Pause.*) That's the reason your marriage . . .

LACI. Vera, will you shut up?

VERA. You seem to have found your voice today.

MARIAN. Not a minute too early.

VERA. Mind your own business.

ROBI. Can I have one more strudel?

VERA. Don't ask; just have one.

ROBI. (*Helps himself to one*) I'll have walnut this time. Thanks. They're really addictive.

MARIAN. I'm sorry for being emotional. When your patient dies . . . (*Pause.*) When your patient dies you feel disappointed . . . let down . . . angry . . .

ROBI. Angry?

MARIAN. Angry. Not with the patient . . . With yourself . . . (*Pause.*) You should have done better.

ROBI. You can't blame yourself.

MARIAN. Can't I?

LACI. You know the answer.

VERA. You're drunk.

MARIAN. Our training hasn't done much to teach us about and accept death. (*Pause.*) As part of life. Tomorrow morning, I'm going to see a widow. Probably with two small children. And I'll have to explain that while I was having a lovely lunch, her husband and the father of her two children died. (*Pause.*) What's worse, she'll offer me money . . .

ROBI. Money?

MARIAN. Have you forgotten? (*Pause.*) Doctors are very poorly paid. Health care is free in principle, but patients are expected to pay. The doctors. The nurses.

ROBI. Yes, I remember. It's called . . .

VERA. *Parasolventia.*

ROBI. Yes. Will you accept it?

MARIAN. Of course not. (*Pause.*) Not from her. (*Pause.*) Medicine was once a vocation and now it's becoming a business.

ROBI. Do you think it's better in the States?

MARIAN. Doctors earn well. Even in England. My ex doesn't complain.

ROBI. The first question they ask at an emergency clinic in the States is: 'Do you have a bank account?'

MARIAN. And this takes us straight back to you, Robi.

ROBI. What do you mean?

MARIAN. All this time you haven't said much about yourself.

VERA. That's quite true.

ROBI. (*Looking at* MARIAN) So, I'm, to use a medical term, up for dissection?

MARIAN. Well, yes.

ROBI. (*Looking at* VERA) Or a cross examination . . .

VERA. Nothing of the sort.

ROBI. . . . . from the State prosecutor . . .

VERA. Robi, you've got this wrong. (*Pause.*) I'm *not* a prosecutor for the State. I'm a judge; that's all.

MARIAN. Isn't there a little bit more to it?

VERA. All I try to do is to serve justice . . .

MARIAN. . . . in the interest of the State.

VERA. Marian, how many times do I have to tell you?

ROBI. Vera, earlier you said you had access to my father's file.

VERA. Yes, I had.

ROBI. Why?

VERA. I told you. (*Pause.*) We were reviewing cases. Is that wrong?

ROBI. No. But would *any* lawyer get access?

VERA. Of course not.

ROBI. So who authorised you?

VERA. If you weren't our guest I would say: Mind your own business.

LACI. (*With irony*) But since you're such an easy going . . .

VERA. Laci, you're really getting drunk.

LACI. I only try to do my best.

ROBI. Sorry, Vera, I didn't want to upset you.

VERA. You haven't. I'll answer your question. (*Pause.*) The Justice Minister. (*Pause.*) And our remit was to identify cases which should be reviewed on the grounds of possible miscarriages of justice.

MARIAN. And this process of yours hasn't brought back to life all those who had been executed by the Communists. (*Pause.*) Including the Prime Minister of the country.

VERA. There weren't too many of those.

MARIAN. Vera, do you know how ridiculous you sound? Not too many innocent people were executed?

VERA. Innocence is not always the opposite of guilt. But let's not digress.

ROBI. So my father was a small fish in a big pond.

VERA. Yes. He was a victim, with many others, whom an insecure regime wanted to get, temporarily, out of the way.

ROBI. Temporarily?

VERA. Yes. Until law and order were restored.

LACI. Your sentence dear Vera should be rephrased: 'Law was suspended while order was restored.'

VERA. About that, you should ask your brother.

(*Silence.*)

LACI. Stop talking about him.

VERA. It was to some extent their mess we had to clean up.

ROBI. My father . . .

VERA. Your father was a simple case. (*Pause.*) His sentence
was quashed.

ROBI. You didn't tell me everything.

(*Silence.*)

VERA. Why do you say that?

ROBI. Before lunch you said something.

VERA. I can't remember.

ROBI. Try.

MARIAN. Can we change the subject?

LACI. Perhaps we should.

(*Silence.*)

VERA. Robi is right. (*Pause.*) I didn't quite finish.

ROBI. You should.

LACI. Are we playing a sort of game?

VERA. No, we aren't. (*Pause.*) I will finish.

ROBI. Please do.

VERA. (*Facing* ROBI) Your father worked for the secret police.

(*Silence.*)

ROBI. What did you say?

VERA. You heard.

MARIAN. It can't be right.

LACI. It must have been a mistake.

VERA. It wasn't.

ROBI. (*Recovering from the shock*) I can't believe it.

VERA. Do you think I lie?

ROBI. I didn't say you do.

VERA. Thank you.

ROBI. Why?

VERA. Why did tens of thousands of people do it? (*Pause.*)
Intimidation. Blackmail. Conviction.

MARIAN. Conviction?

VERA. Yes. The belief the enemy wants to destroy the system in which they believed.

LACI. But Robi's father . . .

ROBI. He wouldn't.

VERA. It isn't as bad, as you think.

ROBI. What do you mean? (*Pause.*) Are there grades of being a police informer?

VERA. Yes. (*Pause.*) Your father didn't work for them for years.

ROBI. What did he do?

VERA. He allowed the police to look at the files of some of his clients.

ROBI. But why?

VERA. He was blackmailed in the early 50s.

ROBI. Blackmailed?

VERA. They said they could charge him with being subversive. They had forged documents against him. (*Pause.*) They threatened him with a trial, and all that would have entailed.

ROBI. Meaning?

VERA. Loss of his practice. (*Pause.*) It might have directly affected you.

ROBI. Me? How?

VERA. They could have prevented you from going to university.

MARIAN. Vera, was it necessary to rake up this old mess?

LACI. I'm amazed. You shouldn't have . . .

VERA. Robi insisted.

LACI. It's unforgivable.

VERA. That's your opinion.

ROBI. It's something I'll have to live with. (*Pause.*) Laci, can I have a little more brandy? I need it.

LACI. (*Pours some brandy into* ROBI's *glass*) With pleasure. I'll join you. (*Pours some into his glass.*) Anybody else?

MARIAN. No thank you.

VERA. I should add . . .

LACI. I think you said enough.

VERA. Will you shut up?!

(LACI *stands up and with the glass in his hand, leaves the room, banging the door behind him.*)

MARIAN. We should have been spared all this.

VERA. Shall I apologise?

ROBI. No need. It's my fault.

MARIAN. Hardly.

ROBI. That explains it.

MARIAN. What?

ROBI. Why my dad was so keen to emigrate.

MARIAN. And you? You wanted to go, didn't you?

ROBI. Yes. For another reason.

MARIAN. What was that?

ROBI. Never mind. (*Pause.*) Vera, shouldn't we call back Laci?

VERA. Yes, we should. I hope his sulking is over. (*She stands up, opens the bedroom the door*) Laci, please come back.

ROBI. (*Shouting*) We want you here.

(LACI *returns with an empty glass without saying a single word.*)

MARIAN. (*to* LACI) Cheer up, old man.

(*Silence.*)

MARIAN. Robi, you still haven't said much about yourself.

ROBI. Haven't I?

LACI. Not really.

ROBI. You know what I do, where I live . . .

VERA. Yes, but not much else.

ROBI. Is there anything you want to know?

MARIAN. Yes. (*Pause.*) Are you happy?

ROBI. Happy? (*Pause.*) It's a big question. Is there an answer?

LACI. You should ask questions which can be answered.

ROBI. I don't know. I'm satisfied.

LACI. It's not quite the same.

ROBI. I know. (*Pause.*) Are you Marian?

MARIAN. No. I'm not.

VERA. You see Laci, the question can be answered.

MARIAN. You said you lived alone.

ROBI. Yes.

MARIAN. Did you always?

ROBI. No.

VERA. Marian, who's doing the cross-examination now?

MARIAN. I'm curious.

(*Silence.*)

ROBI. If you really want to know Marian, I shared my apartment with a young black guy for three years.

(*Silence.*)

MARIAN. Robi, are you gay?

(*Silence.*)

ROBI. It wasn't a sexual relationship.

MARIAN. Should we believe it?

LACI. Marian, you are outrageous.

ROBI. He was one of my junior colleagues at the law firm. A brilliant advocate with a great future. (*Pause.*) He became HIV-positive and developed AIDS. It was early during the epidemic. AIDS was called the gay plague then.

MARIAN. I remember the first cases here. (*Pause.*) Robi, I'm sorry.

(*Silence.*)

LACI. You looked after him?

ROBI. Sort of . . .

MARIAN. Sort of?

ROBI. Between his ever longer stays in hospital. (*Pause.*) His family didn't want to see him, or hear from him.

LACI. Terrible.

ROBI. If you knew his family you might have understood. (*Pause.*) They were deeply religious people, from a southern state.

MARIAN. One would expect their religion . . .

VERA. (*interrupting*) Unfortunately faith and compassion don't always go hand in hand.

ROBI. I had a spare bedroom and asked him to stay with me.

LACI. For how long?

ROBI. Until his death three years ago.

LACI. What was his name?

ROBI. Dean.

MARIAN. How did you cope?

ROBI. It wasn't easy. (*Pause.*) Particularly towards the end.

LACI. You must have been very fond of him.

(*Silence.*)

ROBI. Yes. (*Pause.*) I was.

VERA. I am so sorry. It must have been a terrible experience for you.

ROBI. It was. At the same time it was perhaps the best thing that ever happened to me.

MARIAN. What do you mean?

ROBI. This experience, looking after someone who was dying and who knew he was dying, has changed me.

MARIAN. Changed you?

LACI. In what way?

ROBI. I decided to work for this charity.

VERA. The AIDS one?

ROBI. One day a week. Pro bono.

MARIAN. For the common good. Unpaid.

ROBI. Yes. (*Pause.*) Looking after Dean has opened my eyes.

MARIAN. To what?

ROBI. Difficult to explain. Having a privileged life.

MARIAN. Who has a privileged life?

ROBI. I do.

MARIAN. I wish we did.

ROBI. I know. Working for this charity, I discovered the extraordinary lives some people lead. And in most cases they don't have a choice. Having led a self-indulgent life, I felt an obligation to help.

MARIAN. You sound a wee bit sanctimonious. (*Pause.*) Perhaps I should have gone with you. We both would have had a very different life.

ROBI. Perhaps.

MARIAN. I should go.

ROBI. Please stay.

MARIAN. We should meet again.

ROBI. Why don't you come to visit me in New York?

MARIAN. I don't even have your address.

ROBI. That's easy to remedy. (*He hands a card to* MARIAN.) Here it is. (*Pause.*) And while we're at it . . . (*He hands another card to* LACI.)

MARIAN. (*Looking at the card*) It's a smart address.

VERA. How do you know?

ROBI. It's Upper East Side. Bought it a long time ago. I don't think I could afford it now. It's very convenient. The firm is a short walk away and the Museum is literally next door.

MARIAN. So I may see you next year.

ROBI. Seriously?

MARIAN. Yes.

ROBI. I have a guest bedroom, you know.

MARIAN. It's getting on. I really must go.

VERA. I'll give you a lift.

MARIAN. Don't bother.

VERA. It's no bother. You have to change buses, and on Sundays everything takes longer. By car it's only a few

minutes. If you want I can drop you at the hospital. (*Pause.*)
Laci, where is the car key?

LACI. In the usual . . .

VERA. (*Leaves the room but returns immediately*) It's not on
the hall table.

LACI. (*Searches his trouser pockets and produces the key*)
Sorry, I forgot to put it back.

VERA. You seem to be distracted these days.

MARIAN. Robi, goodbye.

ROBI. See you next year in New York.

MARIAN. If not, here in Budapest.

VERA. I'll be back soon.

(ROBI *and* MARIAN *embrace and kiss each other.* MARIAN
leaves, followed by VERA.)

(ROBI *and* LACI *are sitting in the armchairs, facing each
other.*)

LACI. Suddenly it's getting dark.

ROBI. Yes.

LACI. The days are getting shorter.

ROBI. Yes.

LACI. The autumn is upon us.

ROBI. It's my favourite season.

LACI. It's still outside.

ROBI. Eerily so.

LACI. It's a Sunday evening.

ROBI. Yes.

LACI. Not many people are in the street.

ROBI. They've all gone home.

LACI. Would you like to have a drink?

ROBI. Do you remember the last time we met?

LACI. Yes. (*Pause.*) No.

ROBI. Yes or no?

LACI. I wanted to forget.

ROBI. Did you?

LACI. Not really . . .

ROBI. Can't you remember?

LACI. It's all scrambled up in my mind. (*Pause.*) A mosaic with pieces missing.

ROBI. Why?

LACI. What happened later.

ROBI. It is important you remembered.

LACI. Important?

ROBI. Yes. (*Pause.*) For me.

LACI. I'm sure you're right.

ROBI. What an extraordinary way . . .

LACI. Do you remember?

ROBI. Yes. (*Pause.*) Very well.

LACI. We got drunk at Marian's.

ROBI. Very drunk.

LACI. Yes.

ROBI. We were desperate. Everything seemed to have been lost.

LACI. Yes.

ROBI. We were going to remain a Soviet colony. And so many lives lost in vain.

LACI. Yes.

ROBI. As we left, Marian was crying.

LACI. Yes.

ROBI. Do you know what happened next?

LACI. No.

ROBI. Don't you?

LACI. No.

ROBI. You asked me to stay in your flat for the night.

LACI. Did I?

ROBI. Yes, you did.

LACI. I don't remember.

ROBI. Try.

LACI. I can't.

ROBI. You said I should go with you.

LACI. Did I?

ROBI. Laci, don't pretend.

LACI. I'm not.

ROBI. You said you lived nearby and it would be dangerous for me to go home on my own.

LACI. Did I say that?

ROBI. Yes, you did.

LACI. I don't remember a single thing.

ROBI. It was going to be late. There was no public transport and although the fighting had stopped, the streets weren't safe.

LACI. Yes.

ROBI. Your parents were away in the country, getting food from your aunt . . .

LACI. Yes.

ROBI. . . . and your brother was on night duty.

LACI. Yes.

ROBI. You keep saying yes, but I don't know whether . . .

LACI. I try. (*Pause.*) Believe me, I try so hard.

ROBI. When we arrived everything was dark and silent. (*Pause.*) We went to your room, and drank more. (*Pause.*) I wanted to have a shower, but you said the noise would wake up the neighbours. (*Pause.*) Then we both went to bed. (*Pause.*) To your bed.

(*Silence.*)

ROBI. Do you remember what happened next?

LACI. I don't.

ROBI. You must.

LACI. I don't want to.

ROBI. Laci, look at me. (*Pause.*) You must.

(*Silence.*)

LACI. Yes. (*Pause.*) I remember.

ROBI. What do you remember?

LACI. The light was switched on . . .

ROBI. It was your brother. (*Pause.*) Wasn't it?

LACI. Yes.

ROBI. In full uniform.

LACI. Yes.

(*Silence.*)

ROBI. I sat up in bed, paralysed, not knowing what happened. You were still asleep. He stood in the door for a second, recovering from the surprise, silent. (*Pause.*) Then he started to scream.

LACI. Yes.

ROBI. You woke up. (*Pause.*) Do you know what he screamed?

LACI. Yes. (*Pause.*) No.

ROBI. 'You bloody faggot, get out of my brother's bed, I am going to kill you.'

LACI. Did he say that?

ROBI. He did. (*Pause.*) I'll never forget his face, distorted by hate. I jumped out of the bed, and started to dress. For a minute I was terrified he would kill me. (*Pause.*) But instead, he jumped on you and started to beat you. (*Pause.*) You remember that, don't you?

LACI. Yes, I do.

ROBI. I tried to get him off you, but he was much stronger, and turned against me. He hit me so hard in the head that I fell to the floor. I thought I was going to pass out, but from all fours I stood up. My lip was bleeding from a deep gash. (*Pause.*) You were sitting on the bed, crying.

LACI. Yes. (*Pause.*) And I haven't stopped ever since.

ROBI. What did you say?

LACI. Nothing.

ROBI. I collected my things and as I was leaving, he shouted after me: 'Don't you think it's the end of the story.' (*Pause.*) And it wasn't.

(*The telephone rings.*)

LACI. (*Answers it.*) Yes. (*Pause.*) Yes, I'll pass you to him. (*He hands to receiver to* ROBI.) It's Marian for you.

ROBI. Hi. (*Pause.*) Don't be silly, of course not. (*Pause.*) Me, too. (*Pause.*) I'll tell him. (*He replaces the receiver.*) Marian apologised for asking so many personal questions. (*Pause.*) Vera's on her way back.

(*Silence.*)

ROBI. What happened after I left?

LACI. Another drink?

ROBI. No, thank you.

LACI. I must have one. (*He walks to the tray and pours a large measure.*) Do you want to know?

ROBI. Why do you ask?

LACI. You may not want to hear.

ROBI. I do.

LACI. My brother dragged me out of the bed. Naked. (*Pause.*) And he locked me into the bathroom. He didn't say a single word. (*Pause.*) I banged on the door, until my hands started to bleed. I shouted until no word would come out my mouth. (*Pause.*) Then he left. I heard the door of the flat shut behind him.

ROBI. I'm sorry.

LACI. Are you? (*Pause.*) And then . . . (*He cannot continue.*)

ROBI. And then?

LACI. (*stands up, rolls up his right shirt sleeve and walks to* ROBI.) This is what happened.

ROBI. (*Stands up and looks at* LACI's *arms*) I cannot see in this light.

LACI. (*Switches on the standing lamp behind* ROBI's *armchair*) This is what happened.

ROBI. (*Seeing the scars on* LACI's *wrist*) My God.

(*Silence.*)

ROBI. But why? (*He walks to* LACI *and wants to hug him, but* LACI *steps back.*)

LACI. (*Switches the light off*) Why? (*Pause.*) Humiliation. Shame. Anger. Terror. Confusion. Isn't that enough?

ROBI. I wish I hadn't stayed that night.

LACI. I asked you. (*Pause.*) The next day I was waking up in the Military Hospital.

ROBI. The Military Hospital?

LACI. Yes. (*Pause.*) You forget my brother . . .

ROBI. Of course.

LACI. He came back and found me in the bath. Unconscious. Still naked. (*Pause.*) He saved me.

ROBI. He's your brother.

LACI. Sometimes I wish he didn't.

ROBI. How can you say such a thing?

LACI. I was put under psychiatric observation. (*Pause.*) Locked up. (*Pause.*) Later I was diagnosed with depression.

ROBI. Many people have . . .

LACI. But not many are treated with ECT.

ROBI. They didn't . . .

LACI. Yes, they did.

ROBI. Laci, I need a drink.

LACI. Give me your glass. (*He pours a drink and hands it to* ROBI.)

ROBI. Thank you.

LACI. You can't imagine how dreadful it was. (*Pause.*) They tie you down. They gag you. And then an earthquake erupts in your body. The aftermath is even worse. The pain floods you and you helplessly submerge. When it's over, you feel elation as the pain withdraws but it remains with you like a malignant tumour. You don't know where. In your brain? Heart? Lungs?

ROBI. I wish I had stayed with you.

LACI. But you didn't.

(*Silence.*)

LACI. You didn't tell me what happened after you left our flat.

ROBI. Marian's call interrupted me.

LACI. Carry on.

ROBI. I don't know how I got home. (*Pause.*) But somehow I did. I wanted to clean the blood from my face, but I made it worse. I had to tell my parents what had happened. My mother started to cry. My dad was agitated and threatened to kill your brother, but of course he knew it was just posturing.

LACI. That was all?

ROBI. Not quite. (*Pause.*) The worse was to come.

(*Silence.*)

LACI. Do you know what our country excels in?

ROBI. At a guess: in good musicians and bad politicians?

LACI. In unpleasant surprises.

ROBI. Well, it was an unpleasant surprise.

LACI. What?

ROBI. The next morning I was arrested.

LACI. By?

ROBI. You can guess.

(*Pause.*)

LACI. Did they have a warrant?

ROBI. No. (*Pause.*) They told my father they were arresting me for counter-revolutionary activity.

LACI. Did they have a uniform?

ROBI. No.

LACI. They must have been from State Security.

ROBI. Probably. (*Pause.*) I don't know.

LACI. Did you know where they were taking you?

ROBI. No. In their car they blindfolded me.

LACI. When you arrived, did they remove the blindfold?

ROBI. Yes. But I still didn't have the faintest clue where I was. (*Pause.*) It could have been anywhere.

LACI. Anywhere?

ROBI. A room without any distinguishing features. A table and a couple of chairs. The windows were blackened out. (*Pause.*) There was one odd thing.

LACI. What?

ROBI. There were no lights, despite the electricity having been restored by then.

LACI. It must have been pitch black.

ROBI. No it wasn't. (*Pause.*) There were several large, thick candles.

LACI. Candles?

ROBI. Yes. (*Pause.*) Candles. The ones you could see in churches at better times.

LACI. What happened?

ROBI. The usual.

LACI. The usual?

ROBI. They accused me of counter-revolutionary activity. (*Pause.*) When I denied it, they started to beat me.

LACI. They beat you?

ROBI. Yes. (*Pause.*) Are you surprised?

LACI. What did you say?

ROBI. Does it matter?

LACI. Yes.

ROBI. I said, I didn't kill anybody, didn't hurt anybody and I didn't fight. (*Pause.*) I took part, like so many students, in demonstrations. (*Pause.*) After a while they stopped beating me and left the room.

LACI. Who?

ROBI. The two men who took me from home.

LACI. Did they release you?

ROBI. No. (*Pause.*) I was left in the room on my own. After a while they came back. (*Pause.*) Do you want to hear the rest?

LACI. Yes.

ROBI. They forced me to lie on the table. Face down. They tied my arms and legs with a rope to the table's legs. (*Pause.*) Then they pulled my trousers and pants down. I thought they were going to whip me. But they didn't. After a while someone else came in. No one said a single word. (*Pause.*) Suddenly I felt terrible pain and it took me a few seconds to realise that I was not being flogged. (*Pause.*) I was raped.

LACI. Raped?

ROBI. With a truncheon.

(*Silence.*)

ROBI. Do you know what the worst thing was?

LACI. The humiliation?

ROBI. Knowing who it was.

LACI. Who?

ROBI. Your brother.

(*Silence.*)

LACI. I wish I could say I don't believe you. How did you find out? You couldn't see him.

ROBI. No, I couldn't. (*Pause.*) But I recognised his voice. He had no intention of hiding his identity.

LACI. What did he say?

ROBI. 'You bloody counter-revolutionary faggot.'

(*Silence.*)

LACI. I hope he rots in hell. (*Pause.*) What happened next?

ROBI. They untied me, dragged me to a washbasin and gave me a filthy towel to clean myself up. I tried, but it wasn't easy. My blood was mixed with my shit. (*Pause.*) When they thought I could stand on my feet, they put me in their car and drove me to a deserted dark square. They ordered me to get out and without saying a word drove off. For a while, I couldn't move and didn't know where I was. When

I regained my senses, I started to walk home. (*Pause.*) On the long walk I decided that I would leave this godforsaken country and never, ever return.

LACI. You told your parents?

ROBI. Yes.

LACI. Everything?

ROBI. Yes.

LACI. You were very brave.

ROBI. I told them everything. (*Pause.*) With the exception of one detail.

LACI. What was that?

ROBI. I didn't tell them about your brother.

LACI. Why?

ROBI. I didn't want them to know. (*Pause.*) It might have thrown a shadow over you and our friendship.

(*Silence.*)

LACI. You were my best friend.

ROBI. Were?

LACI. You are.

ROBI. We must drink to that.

LACI. Yes. (*He pours the rest of the bottle into their glass.*)

(*Silence.*)

LACI. Karakol.

ROBI. Karakol? (*Pause.*) Is this the new fashion to say to your health?

LACI. No, it isn't.

ROBI. So what is it?

LACI. Don't you remember?

(VERA *silently enters and listens to the conversation without* LACI *and* ROBI *noticing.*)

ROBI. Should I?

LACI. Yes. You should.

ROBI. Help me.

LACI. Karakol. (*Pause.*) Geography, Robi, geography.

ROBI. Hmmm. It wasn't my strongest subject at school.

LACI. Think.

ROBI. The nearest I get to is Karakum.

LACI. Lukewarm.

ROBI. A desert in Turkmenistan.

LACI. Cold.

ROBI. I give it up.

LACI. A town in Kyrgyzstan.

ROBI. I don't get it.

LACI. Don't you? It's a shame.

ROBI. Why?

LACI. You asked me once: 'Will you come with me to Karakol?'

(*Silence.*)

LACI. Remember?

ROBI. Yes. (*Pause.*) I do.

LACI. Why Karakol?

ROBI. Oh, it was just a whim.

LACI. A whim?

ROBI. The place didn't matter. In the old Baedeker . . .

LACI. Baedeker?

ROBI. The guidebook. (*Pause.*) On the back of the bookshelves I found some of my father's old guidebooks. From before the war. One was about the Silk Route. And turning the pages I found . . .

LACI. But why Karakol?

ROBI. Because it is far away, it has gingerbread cottages and white poplars and no one would know us there.

LACI. Funny.

ROBI. What?

LACI. You, forgetting it. (*Pause.*) The ECT has erased so much from my brain, yet I remembered this.

ROBI. Why?
LACI. When I was treated, I kept repeating it. (*Pause.*) It was
my only tie to reality.

(*Silence.*)

ROBI. I'm sorry, Laci.
LACI. Don't be.

(*Silence.*)

LACI. Robi?
ROBI. Yes.

(*Silence.*)

LACI. Robi, would you like to come with me to Karakol?

(*Suddenly they both notice* VERA. ROBI *is looking at her, but*
LACI *does not move his gaze from* ROBI.)

BLACKOUT